THE
FALSE HOPE
OF GLOBAL
DIVERSIFICATION

THE
FALSE HOPE
OF GLOBAL
DIVERSIFICATION

Confessions of a Portfolio
Management Maverick

MICHAEL ROSS

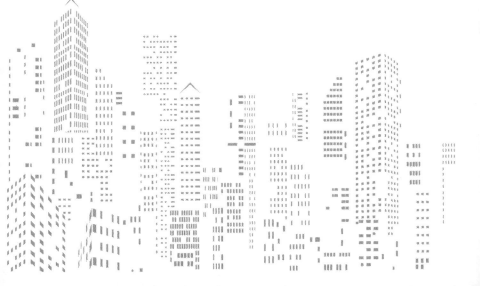

HOUNDSTOOTH
PRESS

THE FALSE HOPE OF GLOBAL DIVERSIFICATION

Confessions of a Portfolio Management Maverick

| ISBN | 978-1-5445-3211-0 | *Paperback* |
| | 978-1-5445-3212-7 | *Ebook* |

CONTENTS

INTRODUCTION

ON OCTOBER 19, 1987, I had been an employee of E. F. Hutton and Company for about nine months. The good news, so it seemed that day, was that I had no clients. The Account Executives, as we were called at the time (the term Financial Advisors came over a decade later), who did have clients, these middle-aged gentlemen who I both respected and envied, were all in a panic. They had seen both their own and their clients' wealth shrink in some cases by over 25 percent in a single day. There was cause for panic! No one really knew that day exactly what had happened.

This environment burned into my brain career philosophies that influence me to this day. Always be prepared for markets to collapse in any one day. Be as honest and direct as possible with clients. Try to be fact-based and be comfortable saying, "I don't know (but I will find out and get back to you.)" when someone asks a question.

However, the crisis that year was also very important to my career development. Over the succeeding months, a series of other financial advisors walked away from my E. F. Hutton branch and left a few of their clients behind. I was lucky enough to keep those clients. I still have some of those families as clients to this day.

The message of the book is that by using our approach, you can *keep* all of those clients who you work so hard and invest so much money attracting as clients. Wall Street banks and the traditional view of financial planning will not help much when—not if—the market drops by 30 percent in a short time. My experience over three-plus decades has been that all of those pressures you feel from traditionalists toward having a globally diversified portfolio will hurt your practice over the arc of your career. This book is written to prove my premise and add a whole bunch of other helpful tips.

THE REVENGE OF THE NERDS

The main characteristics of a portfolio manager are an eye for math, an ear for business, and an ability to persistently learn from one's mistakes. It also helps to have ingrained in you the ability to be stoic in the face of very emotional circumstances.

I left high school with a better feel for History and English than Math and Science. However, attending an engineering-oriented military academy forced me to develop a taste for math in order to survive. Academies also inspire a level of discipline that, at least in the 1970s, didn't necessarily exist in civilian schools.

The Air Force developed in me a level of preparation that continues to force me to prep for the week religiously every Sunday. My kids heard the mantra, "Prior preparation prevents poor performance," constantly growing up. Flying military aircraft—okay, being a navigator even—also creates an instinct to "be afraid to panic."

Another trait developed in my finance career is the need to always address the risk side of markets first. If you can manage the risk, the returns will take care of themselves.

The first few years, when we were called Account Executives or Stockbrokers, I just tried to survive. I was licensed to buy and sell stocks and bonds, options, bonds, mutual funds, insurance, and annuities. I did a little bit of all of those things. I survived.

In December of 1993, the next step of my evolution began. I concluded I needed to be fee-based instead of working daily to earn commissions. Then the main part of my efforts was to bring in clients' assets and consult with them on how to invest, charging an asset-based fee instead of a commission. I believe I was on the leading edge of that trend. As early as the mid-1990s, Wall Street banks realized that financial consultants could help those banks smooth their annual earnings and thus talk analysis into awarding a higher multiple to their stock prices by creating what were and remain known as "wrap programs." The percentage of client assets in these programs is now shouted from the highest treetops by executives of these banks because these fees make the banks' earnings like an annual annuity. I was in on this trend early. In 1994 I began to convert most of my relationships to consulting for an asset-based fee. I chose managers based on my extensive research into their performance.

But alas, my research was for naught! I soon discovered that despite all of my effort and study of asset managers, once I had hired them, they consistently underperformed whatever index I had chosen. This was very depressing. In 1997, after everyone went to bed during a ski trip, I went to the lobby of the hotel we were staying at in Sandy, Utah, and read *What Works on Wall*

Street by James P. O'Shaughnessy and had an epiphany. I could manage portfolios myself! All I had to do was follow his steps.

Back to the office I went, trying to find the data set that would solve all of my problems. In his case, it was a firm's price-to-sales ratio. Here was the silver bullet I was looking for.

Twenty-four years later, I still have the first client to whom I presented my idea, but I now realize there are really no silver bullets.

The pages that follow tell the story of my portfolio management process development and how I began what has become a great career in the financial advice business.

I KNOW YOUR WORLD

AS I SAID IN THE INTRODUCTION, I have been a financial advisor since 1987. I saw the Dow Jones Industrial Average fell 22.6 percent in a single day. This decrease remains the index's largest single-day drop on record. What isn't mentioned often in this statement is that the Dow recovered to a positive annual return by year's end. During the three-plus decades since, I have witnessed six "bear markets" (when the market drops over 30 percent in one short period). During each of these crises, I have had progressively fewer clients panic. If memory serves me correctly, no client bailed out of the market in 2020. My goal is to give you techniques allowing similar outcomes with your clients.

During my entire career, I have been a bit of a continuing education junkie, getting a handful of advanced credentials that have formed my opinions about how to manage clients' money. In the following pages, I will share what I have learned with you. I invite you to spend a weekend reading the book. Please write in the margins, highlight as you wish, and provide me with any feedback that you feel led to give me.

I'll begin with a few observations.

THE LIMITS TO MODERN PORTFOLIO THEORY

Dr. Harry Markowitz earned a Nobel Prize for describing how you can diversify your assets to achieve lower risk while getting higher returns using a variety of assets with different performance cycles. The mathematical language describing this performance cycle diversity is correlation and covariance, and any finance professional must acknowledge that these issues matter. In basic parlance, this means that the investor should spread their assets across multiple asset classes, especially those whose performance cycles vary: when one zigs, the other one zags. *This does, in fact, smooth our year-over-year performance.* It is important for financial planning. It is never perfect, but it does tend to make future asset growth rates more predictable.[1]

Now, stop right there. In the modern world, this concept is taken much, much too far. We want investments that zig and zag considerably from one another, not slightly, but close to 100 percent. Stocks and bonds. Bonds and real estate. Cash and venture capital. You get the idea.

Using Modern Portfolio Theory to justify investing in only slightly non-correlating assets is a waste of time and money. The most important example of this is the correlation between the Standard and Poors' 500, better known as the S&P500, and the Europe, Asia, and Far East Index, better known as the EAFE index. We both know that for your entire career and mine, the traditional financial planning community has pushed you to

---

1   I note this point to emphasize my knowledge at the academic level of modern portfolio theory. I readily admit its theoretical validity when one includes all the underlying assumptions. One flawed assumption is that the investor is objective and rational. I contend that in times of investment stress, this simply isn't the case. Regardless of how well optimized portfolios are toward their stated portfolios—and perhaps because of that optimization—investors panic and make mistakes.

have international diversification, yet that all-import metric, colloquially described as "when one zigs the other zags," or correlation shows that this is false diversification.

When one asset's performance is completely countercyclical to another's, it is said to have a correlation of -1. Naturally, when the correlation is tight, the correlation is +1. **The correlation between the S&P500 and the EAFE index has risen to almost +1 in the last twenty-five years.** Note the following.

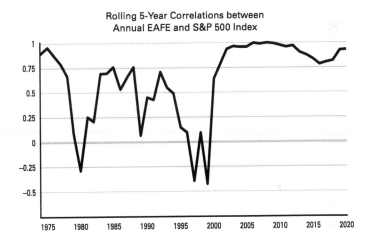

Rolling 5-Year Correlations between Annual EAFE and S&P 500 Index

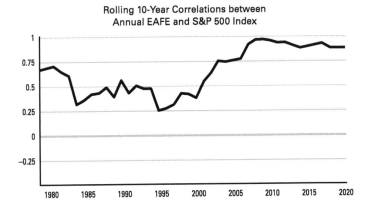

Rolling 10-Year Correlations between Annual EAFE and S&P 500 Index

These are time series of correlations between the Standard and Poor's' 500 and the EAFE (Europe, Asia and Far East Index) of mature, publicly traded companies. These are market capitalization-weighted indices. The "Y" axis is correlation, so when the correlation is "1," these markets are moving in lockstep with each other. Note in the 10-year data set that this really began occurring in the late 1990s into the 2000s. While there is clearly disassociation in the five-year correlations, it almost vanishes in the 10-year data series. Since most advisors tell their clients "you can't time the market" and "we are in this for the long run," why invest anywhere but the United States? You take multiple risks out of the equation and get the same, if not better, performance. Data in this series is from Bloomberg; charts courtesy of Max Grossman.

So with very few exceptions, there has been an incredibly tight correlation between the S&P500 and the EAFE index.

BUT WAIT, THERE'S MORE

As we will cover later, incredulously, China remains considered an "Emerging Market." I know. How is the second-largest economy in the world considered emerging? Can't make this stuff up, folks.

We did the same comparisons between the S&P500 and the Morgan Stanley Capital International (MSCI) Emerging Market index. As you might imagine, the Emerging Market Index is heavily weighted toward China. While this one is clearly much more volatile and not as nearly clear cut, the central tendency provides a meaningfully high correlation again.

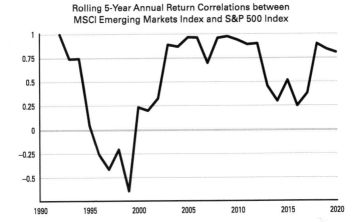

Rolling 5-Year Annual Return Correlations between
MSCI Emerging Markets Index and S&P 500 Index

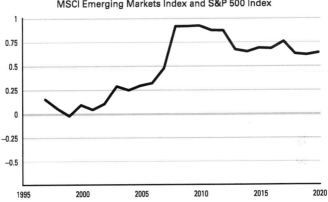

Rolling 10-Year Annual Return Correlations between
MSCI Emerging Markets Index and S&P 500 Index

Noisier than the comparison between the US and mature international markets, This time series of correlations between the Standard and Poor's 500 and the MSCI Emerging Markets index. (Can you believe China, the second largest economy in the world is considered an "Emerging Market?"). Like the previous data sets, these are market capitalization-weighted indices. The "Y" axis is correlation, so when the correlation is "1," these markets are moving in lockstep with each other. While there is clearly disassociation in the five-year correlations, it almost vanishes in the 10-year data series. While the S&P 500 tightened correlations in the mid 1990s, the Emerging markets tightened in the late 2000s. Since most advisors tell their clients "you can't time the market" and "we are in this for the long run," why invest anywhere but the United States? You take multiple risks out of the equation and get the same, if not better performance. Data in this series is from Bloomberg; charts courtesy of Max Grossman.

The conclusion we must draw from these sets of data is that mathematically, as well as logically, the march toward globalization renders all the global stock markets in sync with one another.

Consequentially one really cannot reduce the risk of the equity portion of their portfolio with diversification between different countries or regions. Which begs the question: *why should an American investor "diversify abroad"?*

Also, one must dig into the data to see if this very tight correlation happens all the time. My best examples are the real stock market crises of my career: the 1987 crash, 9/11, and the Global Financial Crisis, to name the most significant. Look closely at all the asset class performance and also just think about it. You will notice and realize intuitively that it was always about liquidity. When—due to investor confidence—there is plenty of supply and demand for stocks or bonds, we all profit. When, really for whatever reason, liquidity vanishes, markets crash. Globally, all markets crash at the same time.

Further, and even more important: all these only minutely non-correlating assets' (like international stocks and small cap growth stocks) movement correlated very tightly during these liquidity crises. This is why markets went down! During those time frames, you received absolutely no benefit from this minuscule number of non-correlations. It just wasn't worth either the effort or the cost of diversification.

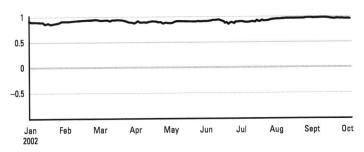

Correlations during Bear Market 2002–01–04 to 2002–10–09

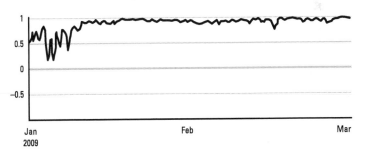

Correlations during Bear Market 2009–01–06 to 2009–03–09

The above charts take data noted in the previous correlation charts and focus on specific "Bear Market" time periods. Again, the correlations are between the Standard and Poor's' 500 and the MSCI EAFE Index. Note that during these periods of extreme market duress, the two indices trade in lockstep, with correlations very, very close to 1. Data courtesy of Bloomberg; charts developed by Max Grossman.

The sheer tragedies of my career were clients who bailed at the bottom of the market because they were scared. They saw their market values go down and quickly turned to some news source. The news source predictably was preaching doom and gloom. They deduced that things were only going to get worse, so they called and sold everything. How did this happen when they were "well-diversified"? It happened because, in times of crisis, liquidity dries up, and every kind of stock goes down.

I have learned in thirty-five years that asset allocation is stocks, bonds, cash, and real estate. Don't use varieties of stock. Consider all those stock asset classes Russell and Associates dreamt up to be one asset class: stock. If you are an accredited investor (more about this later), there should be both public and private equity. Public and private each have risks and rewards, but they are often noncorrelating. This is where you get the diversity bonus; you don't get that diversity bonus by having large cap growth and small cap value, international stock, and emerging market bonds.

Second, own individual stocks with household names. Again, you cannot do this completely because different households have different names, but you can get close. Here's where psychology plays in. If it feels like everything is bad, you might want to sell the market. But will you honestly lose confidence in those companies from whom you buy things? Whether it's Microsoft, Proctor and Gamble, Apple or Costco Wholesale, those companies give you a good feeling which often transcends your crisis mentality about "the market." You relax; you don't panic.

Quick, what is the most expensive part of investing? You say "commissions" or "loads" or "fees," right? Wrong. Way off. The most expensive part of investing is paying taxes. Worse, they are a silent killer.

Volumes of books have been written about investing. More volumes have been written about tax strategy. Like most books, they cover their topics broadly. They aren't custom-fit for every reader. Taxes are very personal; everyone is different. Consider this point: try to avoid taxes whenever possible. When you are forced to pay taxes, try to make them capital gains, preferably long-term capital gains. When you are forced to pay ordinary income taxes, seek to defer them indefinitely. Clearly, there are exceptions to this rule, but begin the analysis with this idea in mind.

This advice is simple but useful. It is also riddled with exceptions that are based on personal experience. No two taxpayers are alike here.

Why do I say silent killer? Because the majority of the US investors invest in mutual funds. I believe an important part of tax management is controlling when you pay taxes. Mutual funds take away that choice.[2] Declaring taxes is their choice, not yours. This is a big price to pay for "diversified investing."

LET'S DRILL DEEPER INTO FEES

Ours is a strange business model; we get compensated by having assets under management that charge a fee or by commissions. Where we really add value, though, are those intangibles like looking at tax issues, dealing with family dynamics, and answering questions that inevitably come up in the press. Our compensation is indirect. While clients are paying for asset management, they are getting investment counselling. Odd, huh.

Make sure you fully disclose the layers of fees. It is common among financial advisors who bundle mutual funds to tell the client their fees. Great. However, full transparency demands you discuss the mutual fund expenses or the manager expenses also. Be

2   Annually, mutual funds distribute capital gains. They decide the amount. You don't.

up front with that. Also, you need to do something similar with annuity contracts. As you know, there are multiple layers of fees. Show that you understand the product by discussing all of them.

POINTS TO PONDER

1. Modern Portfolio Theory, *as it is applied today*, is outdated.
2. Tax strategy is far more important than fee reduction.

TRACK RECORD: NOT THE WAY TO JUDGE PORTFOLIO MANAGER COMPETENCE

For effect, I will tell you my story in 2020. We had a great year; perhaps our best. This was luck, chance, and a modest amount of skill. Back in March, when the S&P500 dropped below its fifty-day Moving Average, we trimmed 5 percent off a fully invested portfolio into cash, as is our custom. When the market dropped below the 200 DMA, our approach was to increase that cash-raise to 15 percent, all the while looking for higher-quality names in underweight sectors in which to buy. This, by the way, is the scariest thing we do; raise cash on one hand and buy low on the other. We will discuss this later in the book.

On that second trim, one approach we considered using is trimming down our overweight's in FANGMAN: Facebook, Amazon, Netflix, Google, Microsoft, Apple, and Nvidia. But, because of the sheer stock price of some of these names then— very high dollars per share—we decided against it. We sold or trimmed other things instead. This wasn't because we had some fundamental belief or knowledge about the pandemic and how it would affect these companies; it was because their share price was high. Since we manage individual accounts with a wide range of sizes, it would disproportionately hurt the smaller accounts.

Is that luck or skill? If you ask me, it was just trying to keep a consistency of holdings amongst a wide range of accounts. But given how the rest of 2020 played out, it looked like a brilliant move.

Make no mistake: while no one would ever admit it, this kind of thing happens all the time amongst the range of professional portfolio managers.

POINT TO PONDER

Don't use a fund's track record to make investment decisions. Dig much deeper.

NO ONE GETS THE MARKET RETURN, OR EVER WILL

There's a fascinating passage in *Skin in the Game* by Nicholas Talib where he notes that "no one can get a market rate of return unless he has infinite pockets and no uncle points." They can't get them because life happens; they need money at the wrong time. They are forced to reduce their risk because of retirement. Or, let's face it, they panic. They take the advice of the wrong person at the wrong time because that person was hired by their bank or an asset manager, was on TV, or had some persuasive argument.

This doesn't mean the investor shouldn't aspire to make some indexes return. Jesse Picunko notes in *Portfolio Management for Private Wealth*, a great book about mixing wealth management with portfolio management, "as professional investors, we need to develop a benchmark[. Having a] benchmark that you can defend as a baseline helps begin the conversation about your investment style." The biggest problem I have seen with the amateur is they have no standards. This very day I have two prospective clients who think they are doing just fine but refuse to reference their account returns—or risks even—to equity markets. They are simply in denial that benchmarking their performance or risk to an index is worth their time. So long as everything is going up, this might make sense. But markets fall, and industry sectors shift in and out of favor. Ignore this at your peril. The perceived cost of advice is trumping risk management.

POINTS TO PONDER

1. View four investable asset classes for serious money: stocks, bonds, real estate, and cash. To spice things up for accredited investors, consider both public and private varieties of stocks, bonds, and real estate. That is all.

2. Be far less sensitive to the investment friction of fees than you are to the investment friction of taxes.

3. Do not put much weight on track record to judge portfolio management competence. Put more weight on understanding the process.

4. No one gets the market return.

Now, understanding these philosophies, enjoy the book! First, let me describe how we manage stock-and-bond portfolios.

IT ALL BEGAN WITH ERISA

The Employee Retirement Income Security Act of 1974 (ERISA) was put into place after Jimmy Hoffa's posse raided the Teamsters pension fund to build Las Vegas, resulting in the creation of an industry that led to American employees of all stripes managing their own retirement funds.[3]

After ERISA came the 401k, built to force employees to manage their own money instead of having a company provide lifetime income after retirement. Retirement investing became a cottage industry that led to consulting gigs by, among others, Frank Russell—originator of the Russel index groups (methodologies resulting from indices to measure US market segments, better tracking the performance of investment managers). With a strong assist by John Bogle (the founder and chief executive of The Vanguard Group and creator of the first index fund), it led to the literal explosion of stock market indices. Fast forward fifty years, and you will find portfolios of Exchange-Traded funds. These funds are a collection of the indices that owe their existence to Frank Russell Associates. Plus, every investment gimmick under the sun.

ERISA led to the explosion of 401ks beginning in the 1970s. Upon retirement, most 401k plan participants want to transfer—"roll over"—their 401k accounts to an IRA. Retirement plans offer other options which encompass several alternatives

3   See more about the history of ERISA here: www.judydiamond.com/blog/ the-history-of-the-employee-retirement-income-savings-act-erisa/.

of guaranteed income for life, but the income levels for these options are so low that many retirees choose to manage their own funds. This chunk of money is generally their largest pool of assets; it's what they depend on to fund retirement and the rest of their lives and then, ultimately, pass on to their heirs.

US Retirement Assets
1974–2006 annually, quarterly from Q1 2007–Q3 2020

$12T

$9T

$6T

$3T

0

1975 1980 1985 1990 2000 2005 2010 2015 2020

$11.3T IRAs

$9.3T Defined Contribution Plans

$6.7T Government Defined Benefit (DB) Plans

$3.4T Private-Sector DB Plans

$2.4T Annuities

Data: Investment Company Institute; Chart: Andrew Witherspoon/Axios

As defined benefit plans began to disappear beginning in the 1990s, American retirees began to manage their retirement money themselves. From this sprouted the boom in discount brokerage as well as the conversion of "Account Executives" at the big banks to "Financial Advisors."

This new cottage industry of "IRA Rollovers" helped create discount brokerages, which offered a Home-Depot-like do-it-yourself approach for the American retiree to manage their own retirement accounts. Naturally, full-service financial advisors working either for the big banks or independently also have participated in this movement. The more complicated the investment options and the tax law become, the more people turn to financial advisors.

All this money swishing around led mutual funds to explode with assets and smaller boutique asset managers, after having a few years of good performance, to launch "separately managed accounts."

Now, marry this tidal wave of IRA Rollover assets with Dr. Markowitz's Portfolio Diversification, demonstrating that you can reduce your risk while keeping your returns high and consistent by diversifying your investments across multiple asset classes. Dr. Markowitz's paper used engineering techniques to find out how much different asset classes varied in their returns over different time periods. His uses of correlation and covariance are taught today to students of all ages as a way to reduce portfolio risk.

So, what American retirees got from ERISA was the ability to manage their assets in retirement. They received from Markowitz a blueprint on how to do this *in the 1950s.*

As I said, it all began with ERISA. Every hallmark legislation in the history of the United States has had unintended consequences, and ERISA was no exception.

I wrote this book to try to persuade young financial advisors to question what they are being taught by traditional educators about investing. Moreover, if you are thoughtful about what follows and actually try to put it into place, I believe you will prevent the biggest risk to your client's retirement income needs: panicking in a bad market and selling out.

By the way, as an extra benefit, you will likely create a level of performance that will help all your clients achieve the comfortable retirement that you seek to have them achieve.

POINTS TO PONDER

1. ERISA led to a generation of investors being forced to make vital decisions on their investment.

2. Traditional financial planning, as is practiced by big bank financial advisors and the financial planning community, is based on approaches that might have worked in the 1950s but aren't nearly as effective today.

ASSET ALLOCATION IS THE FOUNDATION

THE FIRST STEP for any financial planning is asset allocation, but it's not as complicated as you might believe.

The second half of the 20th century brought the financial advice community a host of breakthroughs that should be in the tool kit of every financial advisor. Where the young advisor should be careful, though, is **how each of these breakthroughs has been adapted to fit the narrative of the asset management community.**

In this time frame, a handful of professors at the University of Chicago stood on Professor Markowitz's shoulders, used very robust data sets, and discovered that as the investor changes the asset allocation of a portfolio, the performance differs. Said another way, the portfolio performance doesn't differ based on the choice of one stock or bond versus another as much as what the ratio of stocks to bonds (to cash) is during the studied period.

Playing off of this discovery, farther west at Stanford, another group of professors took an investor's portfolio, subtracted from that portfolio's return percentage the "risk-free rate," generally the return of the ten-year treasury bond, and then, divided that "excess return" by the variance of that portfolio—how much it differs from its average rate of return. You will note that this return-per-unit-of-risk as a metric is an ideal way to compare fund performance. Showcased by its inventor, Bill Sharpe, this metric for judging portfolio performance is now known as a "Sharpe ratio" and seems to be the best way to compare two portfolios' performances.

One of the goals of this book is to help you *retain clients*. Keeping that in mind, let's examine the work of Drs. Amos Kahneman and Daniel Tversky (who are considered the fathers of behavioral finance, a subfield of behavioral economics), which proposes that psychological influences and biases affect the financial behaviors of investors and financial practitioners.[4]

Their work can be summed up in a quote attributed to the legendary basketball player and coach, Larry Bird: "I hate losing more than I like winning."

One of the Kahneman and Tversky precepts is *investors want to avoid the pain of losing money more than they like to embrace the joy of making money.* If you want to keep that client throughout their lives and even the lives of their offspring and other relatives, make an educated guess of the level of account value decline they can stand without panicking and avoid it. One can always become more aggressive over time. But an ill-timed foray into being aggressive and quickly losing market value on your portfolio is an invitation to get fired.

---

4   The critically acclaimed book *Thinking Fast and Slow* was a layman's introduction to their Nobel Prize winning work in this area. Later, an equally good book, *The Undoing Project*, by Michael Lewis, chronicled their lives and relationships. These books are must-reads for anyone who manages money for a living.

POINTS TO PONDER

1. Asset allocation remains the first decision. But it can be applied in a much simpler fashion that is being used today.

2. As you advise clients, always consider how they will react to a bad market. The Sharpe ratio will help you with this.

FINANCIAL PLANNING QUESTIONNAIRES ARE MEANT FOR LAWYERS, NOT CLIENTS

Conventional financial planning, at the big banks and otherwise, begins with having clients fill out a "risk questionnaire." Avoid these. These questionnaires were not developed to help clients articulate their risk capacity. They were developed by the attorneys and risk departments of big banks to avoid lawsuits. Big bank financial advisors force clients to do these questionnaires so that, if markets go down and the client complains, the banks can refer to these rather sterile questionnaires and say to the client, "This is what you told us to do."

BIG BANKS, REGULATORS, AND CLUMSY CLIENT SOLUTIONS

Recognize that Independent Financial Advisors hold an advantageous position in that they have far fewer conflicts of interest than those employed by big banks. Big banks' financial advisors get more scrutiny because they deserve it. They generally sell bank products and have a built-in conflict of interest. This is a key factor behind these risk questionnaires.

The Financial Industry Regulatory Authority (FINRA), as well as the Securities and Exchange Commission (SEC), have enormous jobs. They are tasked to look at the public's best interests in dealing with investment firms.

If you put yourself in either one of their roles, who would you spend most of your time reviewing? If you said *the larger companies, generally big banks that clearly are the lifeblood of our financial system*, you would be correct. The term "too big to fail" lends itself to some thorough oversight.

To control risks, these big banks with thousands of financial advisors have a monstrous task: keeping everyone on the right side of an enormous volume of regulations. This compliance has some tradeoffs for the client, too: clumsy solutions (like these risk questionnaires). Generally, a key tradeoff bank customers face is inflexibility. The big bank says, "Here are our rules, Ms. Client, deal with them." Ms. Client says, "They don't apply to me." The bank says, "It doesn't matter. We need to stay compliant, and we are sorry if our inflexibility towards your needs is an unintended consequence of us maintaining the proper relationships with our regulators."

POINT TO PONDER

It's far better to have a series of in-depth conversations about reacting to account value decline with clients than to have them complete a financial planning questionnaire.

MONTE CARLO ANALYSIS—BETTING WITH MONOPOLY MONEY

You do the client a disservice if you show them a line chart of steady growth, or even some so-called "Monte Carlo" exercise with 1000 predictions—called the probability of success—because those approaches do not fully address the emotions of seeing $1 million going down to $750,000 on the little investment firm app on their phone. To those people who make $250k/year or less, it feels like they just lost a years' salary.

> For twenty years, I had a very sophisticated physician client who was working and then retired. After he retired, he felt like he had no income. As such, he would regularly call me on bad market days, exclaiming that since his $10 million portfolio had declined 2 percent over some short period of time, he had lost the year's income. This persisted, even though every time we met, I showed him that the accounts produced $180,000 of pure income and dividend cash flow for him.

Typically, in financial planning reports, the solution to all problems is having what is espoused as "a diversified portfolio of investments." The reports proscribe the clients to sell certain things that do not fit the narrative prescription of the report and reinvest in things that better "diversify" the portfolio. Cynically, when you do this, the promoted benefit is to reduce your risk via diversification. But the real reason is to invest in asset classes promoted by the firm. Commonly these fit the global diversity theme that I strongly question.

In Chapter One, I noted how Dr. Markowitz's breakthrough on diversification has been taken out of context gradually since the 1970s. Terms like correlation and covariance were intended to indicate wide behavior patterns between the performance cycles of asset classes but they have devolved into such hair-splitting micro-classes as large cap growth, small cap value, and—this is rich—international and emerging markets. Note that China is one of the top five economies on the globe, rivaling the United States, Europe, and Japan; yet, as I teased in Chapter One, shockingly, it is considered an emerging market. I hope I have demonstrated to you that you do not really get any diversification benefit in these cases, but you generally have higher costs.

In my humble opinion, Dr. Markowitz's breakthrough was designed to help investors build portfolios that were, in essence, crashproof. This is no longer the case. Economies are so very globally interrelated that if one goes down, they all go down. Correlation approaches 1; a correlation of −1 indicates a perfect negative correlation, meaning that as one variable goes up, the other goes down. A correlation of +1 indicates a perfect positive correlation, meaning that both variables move in the same direction together.[5]

---

5   Refer to the graphics in the Appendix to see how correlation has increased significantly since the mid 1990s.

POINTS TO PONDER

1. Those fancy graphs in a financial planning report will fail you when the client has lost a year's salary in one bad market day.
2. Monte Carlo is a gambling mecca, not a portfolio illustrator.

TWO-DIMENSIONAL FINANCIAL ADVICE MODELING— PSYCHOLOGY AND TIME

Assuming you agree with the visceral impact of losing "an entire year's salary" in the market, how do you manage to get people to invest their life's savings with you? Three rules:

1. Time horizon

2. Time horizon

3. Time horizon

This is incredibly obvious, but at the risk of confusion: if the client feels like they will begin needing money within a year, leave that money—future income—in cash. In a bad market, heck, leave two years in cash. This addresses the mental leap that one needs to satisfy to keep clients in the market during a bad period. It is tough for anyone to stay invested if every day the value of their assets goes down. Also, try to make sure the overall portfolio income covers their income needs. This may not be possible, but it's an aspiration.

Part of my longevity and strata in the financial advice industry stems from my 1987-crash-inspired desire to avoid subjecting clients to too much market risk, especially early in the relationship. Continuing this risk avoidance theme, let's talk size of client's account. Most young advisors, unless they are inheriting a book of business, long to get big clients. The reasons are obvious: more revenue, more tools in the tool chest,[6] even more gravitas to have bigger rather than smaller clients. The issue with these larger asset pools that you hunger for is that they must be managed more conservatively, which might go against your nature and even the client's nature.

Keeping with the theme of starting the relationship more conservatively, I will often use this story with a new client:

> If you gave me $10,000 and within six months it dropped 10 percent, that's a $1000 loss. For most people of your asset size, that isn't a big deal. If you gave me $100,000, it drops to $90,000. Now it's noticeable, but, again, something you can wrap your brain around. However, if you gave me $1 million and it dropped by 10 percent, that's off $100,000! You are going to fire me.

We use that approach for two reasons: first, to address someone's loss aversion. While a client might not verbalize their discomfort with a certain level of risk, their body language will tell you. Body language is important and will give a key to how they really feel about this. The second reason is that we can always get more aggressive over time. But if we blow them out with losses early, we most likely have lost a client.

---

6   By tools in the toolchest I mean the larger the client, the greater array of items one can sell the client. Stocks and bonds for sure, but also lending, insurance products, and alternative investments that demand a higher net worth.

Said another way—The quip I use when framing a conservative solution is to say, "It's not good for my business if clients give me a dollar, and six months later, I give them back 90 cents."

Another way to persuade a potential client that this conservative approach will actually work for them over time is to first describe a Sharpe ratio and then show them the product of this analysis.

POINT TO PONDER

Always begin the investment blend more conservatively.
You can always get more aggressive once you see
how a client reacts to a bad market.

WATCH YOUR SHARPE RATIOS

As noted above, one of the legends of the investment business, Bill Sharpe, came up with an elegantly simple way to manage risk and reward in planning the return rates for a portfolio of assets. The Sharpe ratio measures the excess return earned over the risk-free rate per unit of volatility. The ratio helps investors determine if higher returns are due to smart investment decisions or taking on too much risk. Two portfolios may have similar returns, but the Sharpe ratio shows which one is taking more risk to attain that return. Higher returns with lower risk are better, and the Sharpe ratio helps investors find that mix.

Sharpe's work helped train another team of academics, Roger Ibbotson and Rex Sinquefield. These two gentlemen are historically famous for a time series of asset class returns showing what stocks, bonds, and (Treasury) bills have returned since the 1920s. As you look at stocks, bonds, and bills discretely over any one decade, you will reject the notion that these return time series are correct, but over the arc of history, reversion to the mean returns is a lifelong reality. These rates of return just don't lie.

Sharpe took the time series of equity market returns, as stated above, and subtracted what is commonly known as a "risk-free rate."[7] He called this the return of the asset class. Next, he used what, in the financial investment world, has become a universal measure of risk, the standard deviation of returns over some time period. (Most accurately, the same time period as the returns.) If you divide the returns by the risk, what do you get? The return per unit of risk, of course.

What do you do with this metric? Plenty. While using track records of funds remains a flawed approach, judging the Sharpe Ratio of one fund against another improves the use of track records as a tool.

More appropriately, though, is using Sharpe ratios as a tool to project a return series of different blends of liquid investments over some period of time. This is a vivid way to show a client what different balances of stock, bonds, and cash have produced, historically, and infer what they might produce in the future.

Rolling Sharpe ratios of different stock and bond mixes help you find an allocation they won't panic out of in down markets, but that meets their growth and income requirements over time.

---

7   The risk-free rate of return is the theoretical rate of return of an investment with zero risk. The risk-free rate represents the interest an investor would expect from an absolutely risk-free investment over a specified period of time. *The ten-year US Treasury bond is a common metric.*

While this exercise is purely hypothetical, it serves the purpose of getting someone comfortable with what a bad year might feel like. I would, then, encourage you to show them what the dollar amount decline might look like in an intra-year downturn and candidly ask, "Can you take this kind of loss without panicking?"

POINT TO PONDER

One of your most useful tools is the Sharpe ratio;
use it early and often.

I'VE LEARNED SOME RULES THE HARD WAY, JUST SO YOU DON'T HAVE TO

In those face-to-face meetings, it is a very bad sign if the client keeps overruling your suggestions. Be cautious. Perhaps because of my experience in the industry, perhaps because I generally do extensive interviewing prior to anything happening, I only give advice after these extensive discussions. I am a directive advisor. If you are being hired to give advice, give advice. "Here is what we are going to do, Mr. Client." If they object, this generally means they think they are better-informed than you are. I have found that when they feel better-informed, generally, their sources are questionable. Be wary.

Do not do multiple choice questions. Do not give them choices. That approach inevitably is trying to put your responsibility on their back. You are being paid too well to shirk that responsibility.

One technique I recently learned from Dr. Moira Somers in *Advice that Sticks* is to ask these clients (who haven't really come around to your approach) is what part of your advice they will have the most trouble with. This might be a precursor to problems that will surface in the future.

Another author worth reading on this subject is Jesse Picunkco. As he notes in *Portfolio Management for Private Wealth*, "A detailed conversation with a client about the financial plan will tease out not just what is possible financially, but what can be tolerated emotionally."

POINT TO PONDER

Client *leadership* is one of your most important roles.
Have a plan and stay with it.

CHANGING ASSET ALLOCATION AS THE RELATIONSHIP EVOLVES

Dave and I began working together in the early 1990s. From day one, Dave was geared for growth. Over the years, we comfortably doubled, even tripled the value of the IRA he wants to live off of once he retires. Two years are ago, Dave came to me, anticipating retirement in 2023. We wanted to move into a more balanced stock and bond arrangement. However, we were not in a big hurry. How do we do that?

If you have a bunch of mutual funds or even a separately managed account, the way you change asset allocations is by switching funds. In that switch, you immediately go from an all-equity portfolio to one that is balanced. Perhaps you don't move things all at once, but you are always forced to make a move. One big move. Likewise, in a Separately Managed Account (SMA). Many annuities offer quarterly "asset allocation rebalances." Most of the big bank trading software for individual portfolio managers has this effortless "reallocate" button. Hit one button: boom, it is done.

I think not.

This is another true story; within our practice, in addition to managing portfolios, we have the occasional retirement plan. Generally, this is a situation where a client simply wants us to handle everything in their investment life, and they are a small business with a retirement plan. There is a range of retirement plan providers with platforms that handle the needs of small businesses quite elegantly. This client's business had such a plan, and we were the "broker of record."

As this client was getting along in age, had a meaningful amount of net worth in the plan, and we had a strong market for a series of years, I suggested he change the allocation in his plan to something much more conservative. He took my advice. *It wasn't a good idea.* The market continued up. (He had been using an S&P500 Index fund.) Two years later, his account had crept up, and his partner, who didn't take my advice and kept his fully invested in the stock market, had meaningfully outperformed him. I looked pretty stupid.

We take an entirely different approach to the accounts we

manage. It's far more elegant than the experience of mutual fund and SMA investors.

Let's go back to Dave. I proposed an idea to him that we regularly use for those in life transition. Later, in the chapter titled "Risk Management," you will see how we raise cash in a weak market: we use modest, and then gradually larger cash raises and—most importantly—buy higher-quality names at low prices as they are offloaded by institutions.

But if we are trying to move from an all-stock arrangement to one that is balanced like we are doing with Dave, we simply do not buy more stock in this scenario. Instead, we buy bonds. *We transition from an all-equity account to a balanced account.* Again, remember your Sharpe ratios. This transition ought to make the account performance more predictable.

This sounds simple, but it is a very elegant way to continue to be growth-oriented in a rising market and then gradually, gradually, go from an all-stock account to one that is balanced. In a good stock market, it could take years! All the while, the account is increasing in size while we "let our winners run."

POINT TO PONDER

Never change portfolio allocation without a market reason. Mechanical allocation tools leave too much appreciation on the table generally.

FORGET "WALL STREET STRATEGISTS"–
THINK YIELD CURVE

There is a cottage industry of forecasting markets. It is meant for entertainment, not for advice.

It began with newsletters, then with radio shows, then with televisions shows, even cable networks. Now websites. There are conferences dedicated to the subject. But, in the immortal words of William Goldman in his Hollywood memoir: "No one knows anything."

It seems useful to hear forecasts, but all too often in my career, I have had clients ask, "What does [insert your favorite bank name] say about the markets?" I am telling you, it's all there for entertainment purposes. Show me one company or one sophisticated investor that bases their real money investment decisions upon a talk from their investment company's "strategist" or "economist," and I will show you an investor who has no investment process. These are almost never accurate. If they are, it's purely by coincidence.

My best story comes from a presentation to a group of top portfolio managers at a previous firm that I had the honor to be chosen to join. The presenter was a well-known "strategist." After the presentation, naturally, there was a Q and A session. One salty old veteran portfolio manager who often said awkward things stuck his hand up in the air and was acknowledged. "[Mr. Strategist], do you actually manage any money?" [Answer] "No." The room was filled with silence.

Ten years later, the successor strategist with my firm did a talk for my partner and me and our clients. In the Q and A session which followed, that strategist with the seven-figure salary—in a weak moment—admitted to the crowd that the best forecaster of future events is "the yield curve."

In 2009, a political forecaster named Nate Silver won a ton of notoriety after predicting the Obama victory. Soon thereafter, Nate came out with a book called *The Signal and the Noise*. The book described how he came up with his predictions. This was a fun book to read, but as important, it was useful to see him showcase his prediction techniques. These techniques he built out over a long and successful forecasting career were the real secret sauce: using that experience to successfully separate the signal from the noise in an election.

The same applies in my world. I would like to believe that I am one of those who have developed techniques to separate the signal from the noise in investing. Let me give you the highlights of a few of them.

SO, WHAT IS THE YIELD CURVE, AND WHY IS IT SO USEFUL?

The most liquid category of securities in the world is the United States Treasury Security Market. Despite criticisms by politically motivated so-called experts, US Treasury bills, notes, and bonds are still considered the literal gold standard of securities with absolutely zero credit risk globally. As such, over the term of maturities, from thirty days to thirty years, the amount of interest one is willing to accept for that period is the secure interest rate. No credit risk. If you create a graph with the "x" axis being time and the "y" axis being interest rates and graph the interest rates of US treasury securities over time from thirty days to thirty years, you can get an idea of what real investors believe interest rates will be over that time span.

Interest rates are very, very closely tied to what both stocks and good-and-services will be priced at over that time frame. As such, yes, the best forecaster of future events isn't that guy reading the teleprompter on TV, the lady on the clever website, or on the radio. It is the yield curve. When short-term rates are higher than long-term rates, a recession is coming.

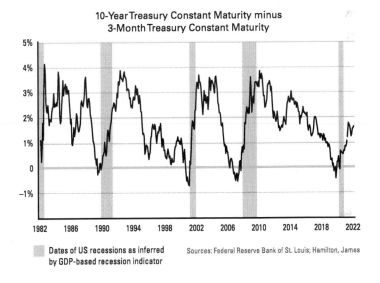

10-Year Treasury Constant Maturity minus
3-Month Treasury Constant Maturity

Dates of US recessions as inferred by GDP-based recession indicator

Sources: Federal Reserve Bank of St. Louis; Hamilton, James

Every time the bold line dives down, it signifies short-term interest rates rising versus longer-term rates. The shaded vertical bars indicate US recessions. Use the yield curve to tell you about poor markets, not some so-called "Strategist"!

Drafting off that concept, there is always speculation about inflation. All of us with the Jimmy Carter Administration still in the cobwebs of our minds think that somehow, some way, that era of high-interest rates will return. This memory is especially poignant when there are budgets deficits and trade deficits to deal with and such.

In addition to the term treasury markets, where you accept a certain fixed interest rate over a term of years, there is also the Inflation-protected treasury market. One of the Clinton Administration's Treasury Secretaries, Robert Rubin, introduced the TIPS market—Treasury Inflation-Protected Securities.[8] The TIPS market offers a series of term bonds where the interest rate is adjusted semi-annually to reflect the CPI-U, the urban consumer price index, or the inflation rate.

If you take the difference between the term treasury, let's say the ten-year US Treasury rate, and the ten-year TIPS rate, that difference in interest rate—or "Treasury to TIPS spread"—is a real-money indicator of what investors are willing to pay, the inflation rate.[9] This Treasury to TIPS spread is what one must pay attention to for forecasting inflation, not what some "strategist" or "economist" says at a cocktail party to impress their company's clients between martinis.

The other great resource in predicting the turning of interest rates is, well, the speeches, minutes, and working papers produced by the Federal Reserve Board. In its attempt to be transparent to securities markets, Fed officials make them available to the press anytime anyone speaks.

These simple metrics are the signals to pay attention to for

8   TIPS are a type of Treasury security issued by the US government. TIPS are indexed to inflation in order to protect investors from a decline in the purchasing power of their money. As inflation rises, TIPS adjust in price to maintain its real value.

9   TIPS spread is the difference in the yields between US Treasury bonds and TIPS and is a useful measure of the market's expectation of future CPI inflation.

the economy, along, perhaps with a few other economic statistics. The rest, frankly, are noise.

POINT TO PONDER

The easier and less expensive the advice, the more you should question its value. Most cheap advice is noise.

PRACTICAL TIPS TO GETTING A BETTER ASSET ALLOCATION DASHBOARD

The flexibility I have now that I did not have for over three decades is refreshing. It allows me to set up portfolios in a way that is more client-friendly and eliminates dozens of extra accounts where they are not needed.

EXAMPLES

- Bob retired from a major oil company and treasured their stock, which he owned in an IRA, primarily for its dividend prowess. He also owned a diversified portfolio of common stocks and bonds that he used to pay out a Required Minimum Distribution from dividends and interest. Big bank solution: have two accounts because, to them, this was a concentrated position that could not be held in whole in a properly diversified account. Independent solution: eliminate one account and have the whole portfolio in one account. Much easier to understand for Bob.

- John inherited a big block of—ironically enough—a big bank's stock. For twenty years, we had used capital gains laws to work down the position. Awkwardly, this necessitated an extra account which, by the way, was charged commissions. Independent solution: put everything in one account, which always eliminated John paying commissions on the sell.

I no longer have to charge clients for things I would have to charge them for at a big bank—like stock commissions for John. Finally, I can limit client expenses to those they need to pay. I don't need big, super fantastic software when it doesn't apply to client needs.

POINT TO PONDER

Regulatory pressure drives much of the big bank advice, not client interests.

Hopefully, you are sold on the universal truth: the first thing you do is choose the asset allocation. What is next?

CHAPTER THREE

SECURITY SELECTION

FIRST, LET'S GET THE MOST controversial part of my belief system out there: there are only four investable asset classes: stocks, bonds, cash, and real estate. In our portfolios, for reasons that might surprise you, we use individual stocks and bonds. Depending on the situation, we use different forms of real estate and then, of course, cash.

I'm a passionate believer of using individual stocks instead of mutual funds or Exchange-Traded Bonds Funds (ETFs). But it's probably not for the reason you think. I believe in this approach because company names will keep people invested in lousy markets due to familiarity bias. We all want to own things we know about.

In every single bear market I have been in (I count six real bear markets since 1987),[10] clients want to "raise cash" just to make sure they will be okay. This is completely understandable. When we collegially scan their holdings to decide what to get rid of, they invariably decide on things in which they have no

---

10   8/25/1987–12/4/1987 (-33.51/101); 3/24/2000–9/21/2001 (-36.77/546); 1/4/2002–10/9/2002 (-33.75/278); 10/9/2007–11/20/2008 (-51.93/408); 1/6/2009–3/9/2009 (-27.62/62); 2/19/2020–3/23/2020 (-33.92/33)

name recognition; this is familiarity bias. If your holdings include ten of the most recognized US companies and also the S&P500 Index ETF, the ETF is going to be sold. It is simply less familiar than those individual names. If you have US holdings and then a various and sundry list of foreign stocks, mutual funds, and ETFs, unless you have some young, inexperienced financial advisor who had drunk their firms Kool-Aid on "owning Japan," "owning Europe," or something similar, those foreign stocks are going. We human beings like things that are familiar to us, especially in times of stress.

POINT TO PONDER

Use familiarity bias in your and your client's favor.
The biggest risk you face as an advisor is having your client
bail out in a market trough.

USE TIMES OF STRESS TO YOUR ADVANTAGE

In addition to being comfortable with holding individual stocks during times of market stress, you can also take advantage of others' emotional reactions. As you know, most stocks are owned by mutual funds, and after that, "Separately Managed Accounts" by well-known portfolio management companies. This gives us individual stock investors a huge advantage. I'll explain.

Credible sources have told me that in times of market trauma, many, many mutual fund owners liquidate their holdings. They panic. Generally, the fund companies that manage these fund holders' money are forced to sell shares of great companies because those are their most liquid holdings. This gives portfolio managers like us an incredible advantage. We can buy these great companies at bargain—read panic—prices. It is also the scariest thing we do. Everywhere the financial press, and generally, the mainstream press, is blaring about how bad things are in the world, and they're only going to get worse. You can't avoid hearing these things; I have tried. You first feel good about your purchase, and then it goes down, and you suffer from buyer's remorse. But alas, you might not have gotten the lowest price, but you have a great price. A wise man once told me that you don't make money when you sell real estate; you make money when you buy it. The same applies to stocks.

In 2008, we thought we were smart as we set limit prices on our buy orders. Every day. It was tedious but effective. We ended up with really low purchase prices. By 2009, this simply didn't work; we were trying to be too cute. Our experience was that those mutual funds that were dumping stocks in 2008 had built out enough cash to be buyers at those low points instead of sellers. We would put very low limit orders on our buys, and the big funds would beat us to the punch. The orders didn't get filled. We went back to simply doing market orders.

So, a key reason we buy individual stocks is to take advantage of name recognition as well as being able to purchase them individually at cheap prices during times of crisis.

POINT TO PONDER

As crass as it sounds, use someone else's panic to profit.

THE CASE FOR BUYING ONLY AMERICAN STOCKS

This argument requires a refresher on topics we have already discussed. First, Nobel Laureate Dr. Harry Markowitz. Remember, Dr. Markowitz's paper was written in 1952. Do I even need to describe how many changes in investing there have been since 1952? Yet you hear the industry soothsayers' constant mantra about investing in all these esoteric asset classes to diversify, as if that, by itself, makes any investor money. In 1952 the entire concept of investing in a portfolio was revolutionary. Heck, it wasn't until 1969 that the industry began tracking international stocks.[11] It was a revolutionary novelty back then. Not so now. Now, there are dozens of mutual funds investing internationally, let alone other instruments.

Now let's do a little study. Let's compare, using five-year rolling periods from 1970 on, comparing what the correlation is between the S&P500 and the EAFE index. Let's demonstrate that the correlations keep getting tighter.[12]

Adding to this argument, if you narrow your focus to exclusively the "bear markets" since the mid-1990s, you will notice that as global indices—the best illustrations of market

---

11   Developed by Morgan Stanley Capital International (MSCI) in 1969, the EAFE Index contains more than 900 stocks from twenty-one countries.

12   See the graphics in the Appendix. Correlations began getting tighter in the mid-1990s. They are extremely tight now. Unfortunately, those who train Financial Advisors didn't get the memo.

performance—begin to weaken, they decline together. They decline synchronously. So when you needed diversity the most, around the September 11, 2001, terrorist attacks, during the Global Financial Crisis, and yes, in 2020 at the beginning of the global pandemic, this concept of diversifying globally has, in every one of those cases, let you down.

Intuitively, now, why is this? You know the answer; it is globalization. In the 2000s, I traveled to China eight years in a row to see a client. Two observations: first, the growth over that time frame was astounding. Second, if I didn't know better, I was simply driving on I-80 west out of New Jersey, looking on the side of the road seeing all of the American brands that had a presence there. So, if these large, multinational companies are doing all of the market research that they do and making capital investments in these foreign countries, why do I need to do thirty minutes of research on a mutual fund that buys international stocks and invest there? More on this later.

Back to Modern Portfolio Theory. MPT achieves its goal if there are distinctly low correlations and covariances. This is a math phrase for our above-discussed point that you need to have one set of assets zigging while the other is zagging to develop more predictable returns. This zig-zag nature with approaching equal returns smooths out the investor's experience.

If, over the last fifty years, those correlations are tightening, why do I need non-US names? Sure, the Asian economic growth—to cite one example—might be greater than the US economy, but to translate that from their local currencies—the Japanese Yen, The Chinese RMB, etc.—to US dollars introduces an entirely new risk. Add to this the possible political problems, and you are starting to have a bundle of unpredictable factors that makes Markowitz's premise, well, outdated.

These risks are more easily mitigated at the company level than by a bunch of mutual fund managers. Former Secretary of State Condoleezza Rice, who like many others has developed a consulting practice with both global political leaders as well as Fortune 500 CEOs, notes in her book *Political Risk* that most global companies have their own departments who spend all their time weighing the risk and reward factors of both buying and selling goods in other countries. They constantly judge political and, therefore, currency risks of their global enterprises.

To reinforce this with a direct statement, a broadly diversified US portfolio likely has 30-40 percent of their sales outside the United States.[13] As a matter of business practice, they have diversified sales; they manage the political risks as well as the currency risks. *Why bother investing internationally if you can take advantage of international growth using US companies while letting them deal with the risks.*

Also, at the risk of being incredibly biased toward investing in America, let's talk about our economic advantages over every other economy in the world.

In *The Accidental Superpower*, Peter Ziehan makes some important observations:

Our Federal Reserve structure allows the US monetary system to react very quickly to crisis. In 2007, Treasury Secretary Hank Paulson was able to pull every key player into one room and hammer out a deal that kept our financial system afloat

13   A 2018 study by S&P states that 29 percent of S&P500 revenues originate in foreign markets. https://www.spglobal.com/spdji/en/documents/research/research-the-impact-of-the-global-economy-on-the-sp-500.pdf

while the European Central Bank took months and months to address that situation.

Likewise, in the spring of 2020, we all witnessed the Fed come to the aid of markets with a series of edicts handed down over a few weeks. The remarkable egress of our economy out of the Pandemic that we are witnessing as I write this book is already proving to be historic. Much of that is due to our globally preeminent Central Bank.

Our ability to trade with both European and Asian Trading Partners almost effortlessly is another factor in our economic superpower status. Should Europe go into a recession, we can easily pivot to working with Asian partners. All must go into a recession for us to do the same.

Also, when thinking of US companies' superiority to their foreign counterparts as investments, we cannot ignore the policing role our media and regulatory agencies play in safety. US companies have to go through rigorous reviews with regulators. Likewise, the media's thorough inspections of potential misdeeds are sometimes misleading, as they tend to find many problems that don't exist. But that is a better alternative than sleeping on the job.

Finally, we have much more of an investor-friendly economy than other countries. This leads to a level of liquidity of US shares that, as was mentioned above, forces the big fund complexes to have to offload large US companies' shares first, simply because when the global economy is frozen up, these are the easiest things to sell.

As I write this book, there are two things that certainly may play out to make this the most prosperous decade in our lifetimes.

To fight the global pandemic, the US central bank is allowing interest rates to be the lowest in a generation. The effect of this for the American worker is the ability to either buy a house because mortgage rates are so low or refinance their existing mortgage loans. The follow-on effects (1) an acute housing shortage that builders are scrambling to fill. (2) For all these new homebuyers, there are so many things to do to improve their houses! (3) For those who have refinanced, they now have an extra hundred, thousand, or two thousand bucks in their pockets to spend every month. And we know that Americans will spend when they can.

Because we are already among the most prosperous nations on earth, it has been clearly demonstrated that our trade policies with other countries might be, well, lenient. Our prowess in creating, mass-producing, and distributing five vaccines will likely be recognized by historians as one of the shrewdest bits of policy the United States has ever undergone. We have a product. Other countries want it. We will give it to them, but. . .what do we get in return? We get leverage in trade agreements. This may never make the news because it is incredibly complex and controversial, but don't be naïve; it is happening.

Do you think I am an investment heretic? I am just getting started.

POINT TO PONDER

Large US companies are the most scrutinized in the world.
Use this to your advantage.

IGNORE THE CONCEPTS OF "GROWTH" AND VALUE"

You have to tip your hat to the consulting Firm born of ERISA, Frank Russell and Associates. They managed to find a business annuity from licensing fees.

There are eleven S&P industry sectors.[14] Where did they come from? S&P convenes what I have heard called a conclave on a regular basis to decide exactly what companies can be in the flagship Index, likewise the Mid-Cap Index and the Small-Cap Index. A committee makes that decision. Then, companies can be classified by SIC (standard industrial classification) codes into industries. I remember reading in the first definitive book about Amazon that Jeff Bezos put an enormous amount of effort into having Amazon classified as an IT company instead of a Consumer Discretionary—books, y'know—in order to juice up the multiple.[15] You can make the assumption that this is what actually led to emphasizing Amazon Web Services (AWS) as a business; it was, and remains, a big tech firm allowing analysts to categorize Amazon differently.

Company executive teams—especially Chief Executives—are judged on the performance of their stock's price. One way to have good performance is to convince Wall Street that you are in a faster-growing sector than they thought you were in. This will lead to an earnings multiple increase which, by definition, leads to a higher stock price.

---

14   The S&P500 is divided into eleven sectors: Communication Services, Consumer Discretionary, Consumer Staples, Energy, Financials, Health Care, Industrials, Materials, Real Estate, Technology, and Utilities.

15   Generally, "multiples" is a generic term for a class of different indicators that can be used to value a stock. A multiple is simply a ratio that is calculated by dividing the market or estimated value of an asset by a specific item on the financial statements.

So, if the S&P's folks handpick the companies and then divide them into industry groups, why not come up with a simpler approach and then, drafting off of Markowitz, make the argument that if you overweight or underweight these groups, you will get better performance than just buying the S&P500 Index? Seems like a way to try to improve portfolio performance while conveniently generating advisory fees, doesn't it?

Hence the Russell Growth and Value Indices were born.[16] Furthermore, the stocks change a bit every year when, on July 1st, the deck is reshuffled, and because of comparative metrics, companies go from value to growth and growth to value.[17] Wall Street Strategists tell their advisors which of these sectors to emphasize growth or value to enhance returns.

Wall Street analysts make an annual game of predicting which companies will switch from value to growth and growth to value because, theoretically, this should cause stock prices to move. (Note that this is also done with additions and deletions from the S&P and Dow indexes for the exact same reasons.)

Now, when you hear your research department suggest overweighting large cap value over growth, or small cap growth over value, you know from where these things came.[18] Russell is a genius! Would it be that tough to say, overweight financials and industrials, or IT and communications services? Probably

---

16   The term Growth and Value also considered the company's capitalization. So, Large Cap Growth and Value, Small Cap Growth and Value and Mid Cap Growth and Value.

17   See more about the Russell US Indexes here: www.ftserussell.com/resources/russell-reconstitution.

18   Even finance godfathers Fama and French found discrepancies between value and growth stock returns over odd years in their research paper "The Value Premium." Some years value outperformed, some years growth. No objective way of forecasting

not, but that isn't part of the conversation anymore; it's growth over value or value over growth. This is the ultimate simplicity. Is there merit to this strategy? Perhaps. This strategy of overweighting growth or value—large or small—and other combinations of groups of stock by their industry or company size has been back-tested to demonstrate that there is merit to these subtle weighting exercises. However, our research has not shown that real people have ever made real money from this type of strategy.

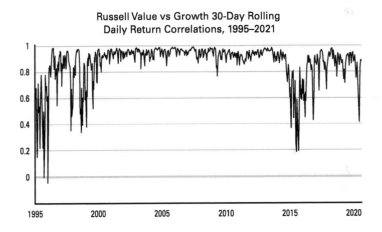

Russell Value vs Growth 30-Day Rolling
Daily Return Correlations, 1995–2021

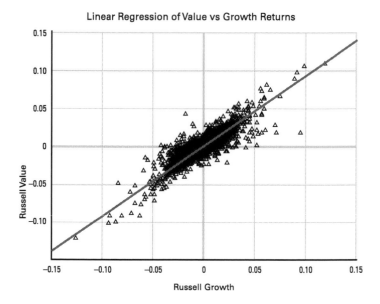

Linear Regression of Value vs Growth Returns

The Russell Growth and Value series continues to be a simplistic way to distinguish between the more cyclical industrial, financial, utility and energy sectors of the market and the more growth-oriented information technology, communications services and healthcare sectors. As both graphs demonstrate, these indices are very tightly correlated. The idea you can gain an advantage by overweighting and underweighting one versus the others requires a level of timing that most advisors simply can't predict. Data from Bloomberg; charts courtesy of Max Grossman.

Back to owning real stocks. If you take a look at the S&P sectors, you realize that, by and large, there are six sectors of the economy that are generally considered value: financials, energy, consumer staples, materials, utilities, and industrials, all cyclical industries. Likewise, IT, telecommunications services, healthcare, and consumer discretionary are considered growth. While there are annual differences based on companies rebuilding their portfolios, these differences happen over time and not magically on the last day of June.

Please join me in concluding there is no real merit in the idea you achieve a greater return in dynamically overweighting and underweighting growth and value. Buy and manage the stocks. Cynics will say their hairsplitting change exercises are primarily there to create commissions in what are generally considered revenue-starved summers on Wall Street.

POINT TO PONDER

Growth and Value oversimplify investing. You're smarter than that. Make sure your clients know it.

FIXED INCOME AND THE RETAIL INVESTOR

Bonds or fixed income really have two purposes for the US individual investor: income and stability. Some will disagree with me. They would say that you might want to own bonds for appreciation. However, in order to achieve appreciation, you must have institutional investor scale. In my view, this requires probably $100 million in assets—owning dozens of different issues and at least several credit analysts. Pension plans, banks, and perhaps hedge funds lend themselves to buying—trading—bonds. These types of investors buy bonds at a premium only to trade out of them before they get close to maturing.[19] They

---

19   Pull to par is the movement of a bond's price toward its face value as it approaches its maturity date. Premium bonds, which trade at a higher price than their face (par) value, will decrease in price as they approach maturity.

perhaps anticipate a credit upgrade and buy before it happens, only to then sell them after the upgrade. They might even buy what is known as "distressed debt" and then sell once the bond returns to something approaching its original issue or "Par price." They buy foreign bonds, thereby making currency and political bets.[20]

Dozens of mutual funds invest in fixed income. This is the easy solution for many financial advisors and do-it-yourself investors. However, to my way of thinking, the risks outweigh the benefits.

Today's incestuous relationship between banks providing financial advice and the asset management business rivals what President Eisenhower referred to in the 1950s as the military-industrial complex. Asset management companies are the servants of wealth management firms. They pay for financial advisors' and even clients' meals. They sponsor events. In many cases, they are divisions of the wealth management firm! These events could be a meal with a speaker. They could be multi-day half recreational events that cost the asset manager hundreds of thousands of dollars to get in the door. Yes, they are, in essence, buying shelf space for their products to be sold to their financial advisors' clients.

A dominant part of many mutual fund complex's product suites is their fixed income funds. These products fit the vast array of "asset classes" that are used to complete what is currently used as the Markowitz asset allocation puzzle pieces. My issue with this approach is that if you use a mutual fund for your

---

20   I really can't overemphasize the burden one has in reading the prospectus. Do not rely on your research department knowing what your client wants!

fixed income, you are immediately taking on principal risk. If instead, you buy the bonds outright, you are clearly taking on credit risk, but absent an investment-grade company having a credit event,[21] that is the only risk to which you expose yourself. You can always patiently wait until the bond matures to collect the principal you have invested.

Our version of buying bonds for income and stability is best demonstrated using the example of the Required Minimum Distribution. It is broadly known that now at seventy-two (in 2020, it changed from seventy and a half to seventy-two), with very few exceptions, investors must begin taking money out of their IRAs. It is sometimes a surprise to people that this begins at only about 4 percent of the IRA's value and very gradually, using IRS mortality tables, increases over the years. It is a modest, albeit taxable amount.

[Note that this same approach can be applied to taxable accounts. If I can approach a 4 percent income stream from a stock and bond portfolio simply taking interest and dividends for the rest of my life, this becomes a very simple way to confidently approach financial planning.]

One of the worst feelings clients have is taking money out of an IRA in a declining stock market. Every month as they consume that money and the account goes down, it feels like their wealth is declining. My experience is that when a client's wealth is declining, they begin to ration consumption. It is psychologically harmful. The idea that people want to spend their last dollar on their deathbed is an urban myth.

---

21   See more about investment-grade bonds here: corporatefinanceinstitute.com/resources/ knowledge/trading-investing/investment-grade-bonds/.

Owning a cluster of mutual funds and pulling capital out of them in your seventies feels bad in a declining market. What if, instead, most or all of those required minimum distributions came from dividends and interest? If my portfolio of stocks and bonds could generate approaching 4 percent-and-growing in interest and dividends, I really don't care that much what market prices are doing because I am not giving up what I might be considering my principal. Worried about inflation? This is where the dividend part comes in; it is extremely common for dividend-paying companies to consistently raise their dividends over time. See the following table showing the dividend growth rate of the S&P 500 since 1989 (data provided by Multpl as of April 2022).

Date	Value
Mar 31, 2022	7.52%
Dec 31, 2021	3.63%
Dec 31, 2020	0.07%
Dec 31, 2019	8.36%
Dec 31, 2018	9.84%
Dec 31, 2017	7.07%
Dec 31, 2016	5.33%
Dec 31, 2015	10.00%
Dec 31, 2014	12.72%
Dec 31, 2013	11.99%
Dec 31, 2012	18.25%
Dec 31, 2011	16.26%

Dec 31, 2010	1.45%
Dec 31, 2009	-21.07%
Dec 31, 2008	2.36%
Dec 31, 2007	11.45%
Dec 31, 2006	12.01%
Dec 31, 2005	14.27%
Dec 31, 2004	11.83%
Dec 31, 2003	8.16%
Dec 31, 2002	2.12%
Dec 31, 2001	-3.26%
Dec 31, 2000	-2.52%
Dec 31, 1999	3.07%
Dec 31, 1998	4.50%
Dec 31, 1997	4.01%
Dec 31, 1996	8.06%
Dec 31, 1995	4.69%
Dec 31, 1994	4.71%
Dec 31, 1993	1.55%
Dec 31, 1992	1.49%
Dec 31, 1991	0.97%
Dec 31, 1990	9.33%
Dec 31, 1989	13.38%

This does two nice things for the investor. First, there is a calming effect of not losing money in bad markets, which inevitably come to the point of saying, *You are only taking out your income from your investments.* In good markets, the accounts generally go up in value. This gives me a great feeling of success as an advisor. To be able to ask consistently every year whether a client needs more income than they are currently taking is a nice feeling.

Let's go back and talk stability again. From the spring of 2020 until 2022 we were living in an environment where interest rates were historically low. Yes, this calls into question the comments about living on dividends and interest, but I still need stability. How much stability? Go back to those Sharpe ratios and sharpen your pencil. This might require a change in asset allocation. This might require more fixed income and different forms of fixed income. What it won't require are those mutual funds.

I will admit I am scarred by the 1980s and 1990s. That era saw the use of fixed income options and futures in mutual funds. If you are being advised to use fixed income mutual funds, remember the phrase a seasoned Wall Street veteran mentioned to me in 2010: "If the yield on the ten-year treasury is 4 percent and you are being offered 8 percent by a fund, you must ask yourself where that extra yield is coming from."

It may come as a shock to you that very few of your peer advisors actually read the prospectus of a mutual fund. Equally shocking, they generally take the discussion of a fund's features at face value from the salesperson who promotes the fund. Like you, they are being shown a lot of funds by various fund companies. Your investment firm is supposedly doing due diligence.[22]

---

22   This is precisely where the risk of the wealth management /asset management company relationships should scare the investor.

If you choose to have your clients invest in a bond fund, read the prospectus. Write down questions. Talk to the fund representative and ask the questions. Be skeptical. If there is trouble, do you really think your firm will come save you?

More concerning are the instruments known as structured investments. While attending a continuing education course at Columbia University in 2009, a Columbia finance professor deconstructed a structured note. Suffice to say, there are risks with all these structured products that many times the advisor is unaware of. Again, your firm is in the business of making a profit if you sell these instruments. These are principal trades, meaning that your investment firm actually built the structured products and has outsized profit margins on them and will clearly profit greatly from your consumption of those structured investments. Please do not take my word for it. Read the prospectus. Write down questions. Ask the questions.

Finally, the structured notes are, for the most part, not really liquid. If you have a need to sell them, watch out for the price you will receive. The difference between the price at which you can buy and the price at which you can sell is a rather large difference.

POINT TO PONDER

Don't fall into the trap of using mutual fund managers to dictate your client's results. Buy the bonds yourself.

CLOSED END FUNDS: ILLIQUIDITY WHEN YOU NEED LIQUIDITY

Another area where I got burned years ago was with an instrument called a closed-end fund. Let me spend a few minutes on closed end funds—some of which we still own.

Idealistically, some Wall Street firm identifies an area of the fixed income market where they see tremendous value but doesn't warrant the traditional open-end fund. They pull offering documents off the shelf and file them. They then market the fund and go to their firm and other Wall Street firms to promote this new fund. While it is indeed much more complicated than this, the real goal is to raise funds, which occurs traditionally via Wall Street firm financial advisors. They sell the fund over a specific time, and their reward is a commission.

Cynically, the process seems a bit different. First, the selling periods of these funds seem to be in the summer on Wall Street when business is slow. This is a way to keep revenues up for firms and advisors. Also, the extraordinary yields these funds produce are by using leverage. This is not unusual. There are many leveraged funds that perform just fine. Third, and perhaps most important, is the fact that soon after these funds go public on the stock exchange, they begin trading at a discount; in other words, the price goes down. This discount is remarkably similar to what the advisor and firm's sales credits were in selling the fund. This is not always true, but it sure seems like it happens often.

Very early in my career, from, say, 1987-2000, I did use these funds off of the initial offerings. However, over the last ten to fifteen years, I began to use them in portfolios we managed. Since the funds were trading at a discount, and we could buy them at prices around the deepest discount, it seemed like a sound strategy. As the size of our portfolios grew, we bought more. Thankfully, though, we bought small percentages of these closed ended funds. More about the small percentage buys later.

One category we chose to buy was oil MLPs. They were great! Using the closed end fund structures, we avoided the K-1 tax documents.[23] We bought them at a discount, and the yield was fantastic.

Then, in December of 2015, when OPEC turned on the spigots and reduced the price of oil to drive the US frackers out of the market, oil prices went down, and so did the oil and gas MLPs. Because these MLP CEFs were limited share offerings and, by definition, had limited liquidity, we were badly hurt on them when we did exit the market. Again, because our exposure to any one issue was modest, portfolios weren't hurt too badly, but boy did we learn a lesson on this. Watch the liquidity of the offering and be prepared to hold on to something if the liquidity dries up periodically.

Okay, after that dirge of cautions about funds and structured products, it would seem useful that I go into a deeper explanation of how we use fixed income.

We buy the underlying bonds ourselves. We buy investment-grade corporate bonds. We buy investment-grade municipal bonds. We also buy preferred stocks at times, but these are trickier. With preferreds, we really need to watch the size of the

---

23   Master Limited Partnerships are alternate investment structures where some form of investment cashflow is returned to the investor. They can invest in a broad variety of different instruments. Generally, the surprise of MLPs to the investor is that instead of getting a 1099 tax form at the end of the year, they get a K-1. This is generally harder to track tax wise and not universally suitable to investors.

issue, the imbedded call, and the call price in mind. In almost every case, we buy these bonds at or below their maturity or call price.

Our luxury is that we are buying these bonds across lots of accounts, all at the same time. First, check the credit rating. Check the price. Check the yield curve, and then buy where we need the bonds.

Where can we get into trouble? Our first concern is default risk. It is always out there. But as an exercise, please do a quick bit of research on the percentage of defaults of US company debt, and you will find it surprisingly low. The biggest scare we have had in the last few years is buying an oil company's debt. Investment-grade just before we bought their bonds, the company made what seemed to many as a knuckle-headed purchase of another oil company. Ratings companies swooped down on this oil company and immediately downgraded its debt to below investment grade. This merited some follow-on research for us.

Three things pulled us out of a jam. First, this particular company had loads of other assets, and over the next few years, everyone knew that they were motivated sellers of those assets. While they couldn't expect to get the best prices from these sells, they could sell them.

Second, this occurred in the first quarter of 2020. As you might recall, the Fed came in with some heroic programs to stabilize the economy during the pandemic. While the pandemic wasn't the cause of this event, the company was helped by the Fed's actions.

The final thing that pulled us out of a jam was our self-imposed diversification. We are only going to buy corporate bonds with accounts where the bond allocation is about $150,000. In a case like this, we might spend $20,000 on any one bond for an individual client's portfolio. While it hurts to see the price go down, so long as it doesn't default, it's not fatal.

Our next check is the price. As mentioned above, we will almost always buy bonds at or below their maturity or call price. There are two reasons for this. One is perception, the other reality. The perception issue is that, while it is generally the case that yields are higher on premium bonds, when a client looks at a statement, the value seems to decrease as they march toward the ultimate maturity. No client likes to look at a value on the statement at a loss. You must trust me on this. If you buy a premium bond, unless you are planning to sell it—which has its own dynamics—it will go down in value as it advances toward its call or maturity price.

Now the final criteria: check the maturity. All throughout my career, I have heard the mantra of "laddering portfolios." Laddering maturities means to buy a series of bonds over time so that regardless of what interest rates do, there will soon be a bond maturing, and one can reinvest the proceeds at the new interest rates. This is cowardly. This also provides the investor with the lowest common denominator in terms of yields.

Instead, simply look at the treasury yield curve. Find the point where you get the most yield for your money and buy bonds clustering around those maturities.[24] The portfolio manager should seek to buy them at par or a discount. If rates go

---

24   Naturally there are other factors that drive our maturity selection in unique cases. If we know a target date we will hover around that date. Since the spring of 2020 we have used very short-term—one- to three-year—maturities believing that the Fed will in some year soon let rates creep up.

up, you know you aren't losing your principal value because you own the bonds and bought them at a good price. Simply trim back some of your stock holdings and reinvest those proceeds in bonds at a higher rate. This isn't too hard of a concept, and you are being opportunistic.

As I said above, we also use preferred stock. These are the closest thing I do to owning a closed end fund now or a low credit-rated bond. Preferred securities are issued primarily by banks, real estate investment trusts (REITs), and utility companies. They are both fixed contracts where you get a contracted amount of income quarterly, or they are adjustable where the amount you get is based upon some interest rate index. As issuers and investment bankers have gotten more creative, there are also hybrids of the two.

We have used them with caution. We are using them because, by and large, they come from highly credit-rated firms, despite the issues being sometimes below investment grade. Are there risks of preferreds suspending their contracted dividends? Just ask a preferred shareholder from PG&E. The answer is yes. It's rare, but it happens.

We have used them because they pay high yields. Why do they pay high yields, you ask? Because there is no set maturity, and if it is set, it's decades away. What they can do is call the loan, meaning give you your money back. This rarely happens. But it does happen. In 2020, multiple issues we owned were called as their issuers were refinancing at lower rates, much the same as people were refinancing their house. Because we oftentimes buy them at a discount, when they are called, it's a nice capital gain.

The two risks we are the most conscious of with preferred stocks are liquidity risk and price risk. Liquidity risk because, like those pesky closed end funds, they are small batches, and if the time comes where we want to sell them, we worry that there will be limited buyers. This leads to the second risk. Remember when I said the yield is high because there are no maturity dates? Well, this means that when the interest rate markets get angry, preferred prices have been known to drop 10-20 percent. This is far more than your garden variety corporate or municipal bond.

POINT TO PONDER

When you do buy bonds for clients, be able to articulate your bond selection process and make sure you abide by it. It can evolve over time, but it needs to be a process.

TAKING OVER FULLY OR PARTIALLY INVESTED PORTFOLIOS: THE BENEFITS OF HUMILITY

Regularly in any given week, we take over management of a client portfolio that has holdings we do not own. We differ dramatically from separately managed accounts in that, with a firm that does exclusively asset management, those holdings are immediately sold. They must be. That firm lives or dies on its track record, and Global Investment Performance Standards (GIPS) rules dictate that all accounts that an investment manager includes in their track record must be GIPS compliant. These firms live or die in their performance-driven world by their track records.

They don't give a hoot about what the customer actually ends up with after taxes; they care about their track record!

We do not, nor will we likely ever, seek to be GIPS-compliant. We are first and foremost financial advisors.

Back to taking over accounts with holdings that we don't hold anywhere in our portfolios, a.k.a. "Non-Model Holdings" to us.

First, in taxable accounts, there are possible tax implications to deal with. We will generally ask for the clients' tax returns to find out whether they have any tax-loss-carryforwards to use. You would be amazed at how many very sophisticated investors do not know the answer to this question. (And also, how few advisors ask to see tax returns.) From this, we will know how much we can sell without triggering capital gains tax and even what the impact is of creating capital gains.

Next, again in taxable accounts, we will sell anything they have to create a capital loss. These will be valuable over the years, if not immediately. Here's where we might get flak from accountants we don't know. The accountant will often attribute a capital loss to a bad investment. On the contrary! Taking losses allows us to take gains later without the guilt of creating capital gains taxes for clients.

POINT TO PONDER

Even if you really, really like your model portfolio, make sure you are humble enough to account for other positions.

MAINTAINING QUALITY CONTROL AND DEALING WITH NON-MODEL HOLDINGS: CONCENTRATED POSITIONS AND OUR GRADUAL BUY PROCESS

Investment managers who run separately managed accounts have it easy. They create a model portfolio where they have established a GIPS-compliant strong track record. This portfolio and its track record is their goose that laid the golden egg. They can market that track record, well, until it turns bad. Then they bring out another fund that they have had in development and market it. The shareholders in the old fund either stay or go, but so long as they stay—many times out of pure inertia—the asset manager keeps getting fees every month. They keep managing it, but their team of salespeople is off to the races with a different "extraordinary fund."

Our approach is different in that we might keep much of what the client has brought to us, we "manage around" low-cost-basis stock and concentrated positions, and we try to pragmatically manage the tax burden. Despite all of these conditions, we are tasked to, and expect to, manage the client's assets to a certain standard of performance. We manage to a benchmark or a cocktail of benchmarks.

To do this, we have several ongoing and never-ending quality control steps.

- Non-model holdings. As I said earlier, unlike a separate account manager, we do not just, as a matter of procedure, sell holdings that do not line up with our model. There are indeed conditions where we sell them, but it's not our go-to approach like others, especially SMAs. To maintain quality control, we review these stocks and mutual funds regularly to try to ensure that they do not break down technically.[25]

- Concentrated positions. I am not a fan of keeping more than 7 ½ percent of any one stock in someone's portfolio.[26] As such, we review monthly all of our concentrated positions. This is not to say we study their fundamental characteristics. This is to say that we review the price of the stock versus history to see if the value is declining. If it is, we review the tax implications of their selling or trimming it.

- Mutual funds. Our preference is to get rid of every fund. Often, though, that isn't the best idea because of tax issues. So instead, we have a series of metrics we look at objectively.[27] Should a majority of those metrics be negative, we work to sell the funds.

Performance. Our goal is always to have very consistent performance across all of the accounts in our model. However, when you are taking on non-model holdings, this might be difficult. To address this, we look at performance in a model over a series of time frames statistically. Should one account deviate from the broader number of accounts in that model, we will review it and make a decision on what it might have in it that needs to be trimmed.

---

25   "Breaking down technically" is another term for the stock price declining through the stock's resistance.

26   The math is pretty conclusive: all things being equal, a 10 percent position in decline will generally have a really negative effect on the portfolio. A 7 ½ percent position will hurt, but not nearly as much.

27   Metrics might include: Morningstar ratings (supposedly forward-looking), manager performance deciles, track redords over the last three years, and comparisons of index benchmarks, historically.

So often, prospective clients will ask about track record. The steps above seem like a way to dodge the question. They are not. We are not a mutual fund nor an SMA, nor do we choose to ever be one of those products. As such, giving someone an accurate "track record" is dishonest.

POINT TO PONDER

Mutual fund portfolio managers and SMA managers care little about the client; they care about their fund's track record.

MAINTAIN SECTOR DISCIPLINE

Dorsey Wright and Associates did a study years ago that remains true. The biggest driver of a stock's return is the market (50 percent). Next is their sector (30 percent). Finally, their individual stock performance (20 percent). This shouldn't be taken lightly. Over the years of my career, I have heard scores of arguments from my colleagues about the unique performance of individual companies in the same sector. While this remains a reality in short-term intervals, it generally doesn't hold water over time.

There are multiple reasons for this. With very rare exceptions, it is quite difficult to dominate an industry over time. A company that has a unique product often finds that uniqueness duplicated or even improved somehow by another. Executives get poached by the competition constantly to repeat at company B what company A was doing. There are armies of intellectual property attorneys plying their trade to both protect a company secret and steal a company secret. As such, stocks in a sector tend to revert to similar earnings patterns and company performance.

I nostalgically remember my old firm holding what were known as "Top Producer" meetings for portfolio managers. In 1999, I was having dinner at one of these functions and sat next to someone new to the group. In the course of the evening, he told me—bragged?—that his portfolio, which had performed so well, was 30 percent invested in one company, Cisco Systems. Remember, this was 1999. I never saw this guy again at a meeting. That one position was not only too big from an individual security position, it blew out the entire sector's weighting.

Face it, managing portfolios isn't really about trying to get great returns; it is about controlling risk. One key way to control risk is to pay attention to sector weightings.

This is yet another reason that track records stink as a selection criteria. How did that wonderful portfolio manager team get that great track record? Did they own the proverbial 30 percent Cisco like my colleague did? Did he buy options on Cisco? Believe it or not, mutual funds are quite opaque, despite what the rating agencies say.

POINT TO PONDER

Never, ever fall in love with your stocks.
They are a tool, not a solution.

BE MARKET-SENSITIVE INSTEAD OF MECHANICAL IN YOUR SECTOR DISCIPLINE AND ASSET ALLOCATION

In my three-decade-plus career, I have encountered many, many do-it-yourself individual investors who pay little attention to sector discipline or performance benchmarking. This is usually proven if they are willing to show us their holdings. We scrutinize the portfolio and discover that (1) When compared to the appropriate benchmark, it is lagging badly, or (2) they have some kind of concentration that presents enormous risk to the portfolio that is only seen when that sector goes out of favor.

Maintaining sector discipline is really quite simple, but it's not easy. We maintain a model portfolio and every month consciously check the sector weights of that portfolio. Note that I did not say correct these sector weights. I said know the risks, so when a situation comes along, you can manage the risks. Why create capital gains if you do not need to?

POINT TO PONDER

Objectivity in portfolio management requires a standard.
The index is the standard.

MANAGING CAPITAL GAINS AND LOSSES

My mantra: best choice, avoid all taxes; second-best choice, pay capital gains rates—here or in the future; third-choice, pay ordinary income taxes, but do it strategically when possible.

Corollary to my mantra: seek capital losses and husband them whenever you can. Whenever we take over a taxable portfolio from another advisor and the account has plenty of stock, the first thing we do is sell everything that is at a loss. Even if we hold the same position in our models, we sell it. Why? We can always buy back the stock after thirty-one days, but those losses are precious.

One of our most impressive achievements over the last twenty years was taking over a client account in 2002 that had over $400,000 in tax loss carryforwards. Among the best tax breaks for an investor is the ability in the current US tax code to carry-forward losses for an entire lifetime. But they do not extend past one lifetime. Sadly, the account owner passed away earlier this year, but at that point, they had only $25,000 in losses carried forward. What an achievement!

So, we deal with capital gains as follows:

1. We husband capital losses whenever possible.

2. When risk management dictates raising cash in a portfolio, we make every attempt to do that by taking losses.

3. Alas, when we need to trim, and everything is at a gain, we take those gains hoping there will be another occasion during that calendar year to take losses to wash out that gain.

Note: you should be engaged with clients continuously. Part of that conversation (that most advisors don't generally ask) is whether the client has any loss-carryforwards from previous years on their tax returns. Ask that questions and keep track of the answer.

Getting back to the main question of this section: know where you are placing your bets. Asset allocation is an easy bet to monitor. Sector allocation is a bit harder, but it can clearly be done. Note that I am not advocating taking immediate action. I am advocating knowing where the bets are so I can manage it in points of stress.

I was in a client meeting at a restaurant yesterday and overheard a conversation, most likely from a mutual fund vendor behind me. He confidently told his audience that his portfolios were reallocated between stocks and bonds on the calendar quarter. While this seems quite consistent and efficient, it is not very tactical. I'm sure this doesn't come as a shock to the reader that markets don't pull back regularly on the calendar quarter. In fact, it is quite unpredictable. Use those occasions of pullback as your opportunities to readjust capital gains instead of routinely doing it on the calendar quarter. This will eliminate a lot of capital gains and might actually make you some money.

Okay, you say, I understand why it's important to maintain sector discipline. The big question is, *what are the sector weights to which I should pay attention?*

You know the answer to this. It's the benchmark. If you are managing to the S&P500, use that indices sector weightings. Ifs it's another index, by all means, use that index sector weightings.

Two cautionary comments: be aware of your deviations, but don't fanatically keep those weightings held all of the time. We try to always know what bets we are making, but we will usually use a market pullback to trim back a sector or a unique client need for cash to trim securities. We will need to be raising cash at that point. Why not use it as an occasion to realign the sectors closer to their appropriate weights?

Next, come up with a variance with which you are comfortable. For a few years, we collaborated with a bond manager. We were managing balanced portfolios together. To avoid constantly getting in each other's way on portfolio management, we agreed that our weightings could have a variance of 5 percent from target. Take an approach like that. Many times, as you can imagine, that variance shows up because a particular sector is strong. Let it run for a while! But when risk management dictates a cash raise, make sure that sector is the target of the raise.

I have already mentioned my best example of this approach. In the spring of 2020, when we raised cash, we left the high-priced stocks alone because they were going to be hard to trim in smaller accounts, and we wanted to maintain consistency of portfolios. Fortunately—here's that "luck or skill" thing again—those sectors: consumer discretionary, IT, and communications services profited most from the mid-2020 market upturn, and we looked really good.

POINT TO PONDER

There is no real answer to whether it's luck or skill.

CHAPTER FOUR

RISK MANAGEMENT

SOME FLAWED APPROACHES I HAVE OBSERVED IN MY LIFE

- Too much cash: building up a load of cash for, in the words of Forrest Gump, "no particular reason." I have seen many, many cases where an investor simply lets cash build up. They are a specialist in one area, and because they aren't open-minded enough to view other approaches, it just sits there.

- Lack of collegiality among financial advisors: don't make the assumptions that because you are licensed to do insurance or mortgages that, because of your close relationship with the client, you ought to do that business for them. Seek other professionals who have high competence in that area and steer clients that way.

- Overconcentrating your holdings in one particular invest-ment or even asset class is a recipe for disaster. This holds true for individuals, for investment firms, and for businesses.

HEDGING YOUR BETS AT THE MACRO LEVEL

Remember the four food groups, er, investable asset classes for serious money: stocks, bonds, cash, and real estate.

To my way of thinking, once your clients have built up assets, stocks, bonds, cash, real estate, and even a business or two, life for them, and for you as an advisor, becomes an exercise of asset management. The key to asset management is hedging risks.

A useful quote from Jesse Picunko:

"Portfolio management is a persistent process that begins with identifying problems that investment assets can solve follows through with thoughtful design and continues forever with a monitoring evaluating and management regime."[28]

Stocks and bonds are very liquid, which works for you in terms of short-term needs, both as collateral and the ability to move fast when necessary. The drawback to that liquidity, of course, is that there is always the threat of almost immediate value drops. If you have used your stock and bond holdings as collateral, this heightens the possibility of a forced sell.

How do you judge your portfolio's performance? On your stock and bond portions, use some index(es) as an expected return reference point.

Stocks are generally efficient. Markets have known rates of return.[29] The key here is to use those performance benchmarks

---

28   Jesse Picunko, *Portfolio Management for Private Wealth*.

29   See information in Chapter Two on the *Ibbotson Sinquefield Times* series: "Stocks, Bonds and Bills."

to honestly judge results and get the client to buy into this form of review.

My most recent example is the gentleman who came to me a few years ago and said he wanted his assets to grow. My first mistake was to not insist I knew what standard he was judging me on, and when he wouldn't tell me, just back away from the arrangement. He was going to compare our performance to some arbitrary standard of which I had no knowledge. My second mistake was when I recommended a particular approach that he overruled because (enter reason here), and I did not back away from the situation. Then he had all of these funky ways he wanted to monitor and judge our performance by the price of apples when he, in fact, owned oranges. (Hopefully, you picked up the analogy here.) The message is to pick an index or a cocktail of indices and objectively judge your returns by that index.

Bonds, too, are priced toward efficiencies. However, one thing to remember with bonds is that they are still an over-the-counter transaction with plenty of possible human error or input. Bonds can easily be mispriced during periods of inefficiency, if only just for a few days.

[The most surprising mispricing is with ETFs. The surprise is because ETFs are touted to be so very efficient. However, during the 2008-2010 Financial Crisis, as well as a few other times, because of bond mispricing, there were wide intra-day gaps between many Bond ETFs bid and offer prices. If you are opportunistic, you can take advantage of this, but you have to move quickly.]

This is a tremendous segue to real estate. No one recognizes the value of real estate investments more than I do.[30] One reason is that real estate is priced less efficiently than stocks and bonds., and the astute investor can capitalize on that inefficiency. Anyone in that business knows how real estate is likely the most inefficient of the four referenced asset classes to buy. Also, once they buy it, your client most likely has to engage in its management. You either have to care for real estate, or you have to hire someone to do that. This could include dealing with renters, property managers, accountants, and attorneys. None of this is designed to discourage real estate ownership. On the contrary, there is a range of ways to purchase different varieties of real estate that will benefit the investor. Two examples:

- Residential properties. I have dealt with many, many successful properties owners who built their legacy by buying and renting properties. The most lucrative were the really hands-on folks who did all the work themselves. As they aged, they handed off different tasks to others, but it was clearly a do-it-yourself deal.

- Commercial properties. My experience is that this is a much more nuanced skill set. Those I know who have been successful here had the help of commercial real estate brokers and others. There is regular work dealing with tenants here also, but it is a nice way to build wealth. An additional bonus is for

---

30   There are tons of good books on the merits of real estate investing. I will defer to the reader to pursue the finer points of real estate investment.

the business owner to personally buy the property and then have their business rent from them. There are complexities with this approach, but there are even more benefits.

POINT TO PONDER

As your client accumulates assets, stocks and bonds become simply one leg of the stool. Help them with all three or four legs. That's what you do when you're a financial advisor.

RISK MANAGEMENT IN STOCK PORTFOLIO MANAGEMENT

There's an old story about a stock portfolio manager being interviewed by the media after a great year of performance. She was asked, "How were you able to make such good portfolio management decisions?" She replied, "Experience." The obvious next question was: "How did you gain such great experience?" She replied, "Making bad decisions."

In December of 2022, I will have been actively managing client stock and bond portfolios for twenty-five years. In that span, I have gained a ton of experience. My team collectively has been managing portfolios for some fifty years. Let me spend some time telling you how we made the mistakes that gave us some level of success.

Let me begin with process. The subject of this book is our process of managing portfolios. Our process has been developed over almost twenty-five years, but we constantly reevaluate it in light of new circumstances, new systems possibilities, and new goals. At its core, though, is a process that has delivered results over time.

One must always begin with a benchmark to follow. Without a benchmark, you don't know how you are doing. Note that this doesn't mean you have to mimic that benchmark. In fact, I would caution against managing too closely to a benchmark because, in many cases, that can hurt the client experience.

Our approach is to use the benchmark with a wide diversity and a very long-term track record of including a wide range of well-recognized names. Remember above when I referred to using "Familiarity Bias" to keep people invested. Naturally, this is the S&P500 for stocks and the Barclays Agg as the bond index.

Our approach is to try to get index returns with less risk. I know, again, with the emphasis on risk.[31] Remember, this book isn't about getting better-than-market returns. This book is about retaining clients.

Let's define risk. The Wall Street folks define risk using Harry Markowitz's approach, calling it volatility. They throw a "statistically significant" number of performance observations on a chart and come up with a variance—meaning how wide of a range is there from the average return over that time period to its largest and smallest data points.[32] They throw around terms like "High Vol" and "Low Vol," which refer to high and low

---

31   We seek to achieve S&P500 Index-like returns with shallower downturns—read volatility—than that Index through raising cash and reinvesting what we have raised at opportune times.

32   Otherwise known as regression analysis, it is a powerful statistical method that allows you to examine the relationship between two or more variables of interest. While there are many types of regression analysis, at their core they all examine the influence of one or more independent variables on a dependent variable.

volatility. Heck, they have created and sold the public investments that simply quantify this term called "Vol."

Perhaps a better way to communicate this concept is with the term *predictability*. Most investors are trying to achieve some rate of return over a specific time period. We know historically from the Ibbotson data set what markets will return; we just don't know when they will have those returns. Market performance is unpredictable.

To my way of thinking, risk is going busted. Your money goes away. It's worthless.

But if one is invested in a properly diversified stock portfolio, what we seek is as much predictability as possible. This is a different goal.

Taking this thought a step further, the risk is that during a down market, your client will need to pull capital out, selling assets at distressed prices instead of waiting for the imminent bounce. This panic selling potential is another form of risk.

Lack of predictability says it will happen over a specific period, not in the next week, month, or year. The returns will happen, but I can't predict when. If you are patient and wait, the market will get healthy. Bear markets in the United States last from six to twenty-four months. Be patient.

As advisors and portfolio managers, we are trying to give an investor the highest probability possible that their risky portfolio will produce outcomes greater than their savings accounts over time. As I stated before, we encourage the use of multiple asset classes—stock, bonds, and private equity if possible—and we try to gauge the risk and returns of each. Bonds are pretty clear cut: an interest rate and a period of time. Stocks have better returns, but they are less predictable.

So we use our Sharpe ratio study to assess the blend. We have a portfolio of stocks instead of an index because the stock approach will keep people in the game during bad markets— which are inevitable.

Remember our approach to managing stock and bond portfolios: first, asset allocation; then, sector discipline; now, picking stocks.

In the mid-to-late 2000s, when I was trying to work my way through the Chartered Financial Analyst curriculum, I also had access to a wide range of Wall Street research. My study partners also were securities analysts.

Among the many things I learned was that every analyst has a franchise. Somewhere in their education, they developed what they believed was the best way to analyze stocks in their sector. This could have been from attending conferences, from doing plant and factory visits, from developing a good relationship with the executive suite, or from doing a bunch of surveys. This list goes on and on. None of these are bad approaches. But none are superior either. They are a mosaic of different approaches that, when combined, can give an increasingly high confidence level that someone is right. Realizing this, I simply became a collector of high conviction buy lists. My bias was the larger firms because they had more analysis with better resources to burn on research and more young analysts to whom the analysts could give the tedious jobs.[33]

---

33   Most big banks' research departments hire tons of interns from great colleges. This is a win-win. The interns get great experience over the summer and the banks' research departments get the pick of the litter when they are ready to hire. These young analysts work tirelessly for more senior analysts while learning a particular industry niche. Each of these senior analysts delegate the more tedious tasks of their particular approach to those juniors.

When the time came to add stocks to our portfolios, I literally looked down my lists of high conviction buy lists and found consensus. I want many firms and analysts to have high conviction buy ratings using as many approaches as possible.

Next came the technical analysis approach. The 2000-2002 dot com bust was tough on me. I had two basic problems; prior to about 2002, when I initiated a position, I invested 5 percent of the portfolio in it. Right away. I learned this technique from a very popular portfolio manager who worked for our firm. This limited any portfolio to twenty positions, obviously. The PM I copied had in the past five to ten years been either lucky or good because his track record doing this was fantastic. I adopted this in 2000 with decidedly less than fantastic results.

The other issue was when I would buy the stock. I would try to purchase in a market downdraft, but in almost every situation during that era, stocks kept going down!

Right after the 2000-2002 bear market, the firm I was working at then got all of us subscriptions to a technical analysis firm called Dorsey Wright, which showcased an approach called "Point and Figure" charting. Starting my purchases at the proscribed time for point-and-figure users was a great improvement for me.

Also, and unrelated, I bought and read George Soros' book, *The Alchemy of Finance*.[34] Soros described much of what made him a great investor. A meaningful part of this is the

---

34   In 1986, George Soros wrote a very challenging book that outlined his approach to investment management—an approach that had provided investors in his Quantum Fund extraordinary returns over the eighteen prior years. The book was challenging in two senses. For one thing, it claimed that financial orthodoxy (as still taught) rests on false premises, and for another, it argued that the philosophical underpinnings of the success of the scientific method could be used to illuminate "historical processes," of which the financial markets are a minor subset.

Theory of Reflexivity.[35] Much of it simply didn't apply to what I was doing. But one point stuck in my mind. This theory of reflexivity prompted a technique he used involving adding to a stock position once the stock goes through resistance.[36] Going into the 2008 downturn, we would initiate a position with more like a 1-2 percent investment and add more if a stock pushed through what I felt was a resistance level on a candlestick chart.[37]

We made another improvement during that time frame. We would begin our daily run-through holdings with the point-and-figure charts I referenced above, then apply another kind of

35   Reflexivity is a theory that argues positive feedback loops between expectations and economic fundamentals can cause price trends that substantially and persistently deviate from equilibrium prices. Reflexivity's primary proponent is George Soros, who credits it with much of his success as an investor. Soros believes that reflexivity contradicts most of mainstream economic theory. Source: Investopedia

36   The concepts of trading level support and resistance are undoubtedly two of the most highly discussed attributes of technical analysis. Part of analyzing chart patterns, these terms are used by traders to refer to price levels on charts that tend to act as barriers, preventing the price of an asset from getting pushed in a certain direction. Technical analysts use support and resistance levels to identify price points on a chart where the probabilities favor a pause or reversal of a prevailing trend. Support occurs where a downtrend is expected to pause due to a concentration of demand. Resistance occurs where an uptrend is expected to pause temporarily, due to a concentration of supply. See Investopedia: https://www.investopedia.com/terms/s/support.asp and https://www.investopedia.com/terms/r/resistance.asp.

37   Candlestick charts originated in Japan over 100 years before the West developed the bar and point-and-figure charts. In the 1700s, a Japanese man named Homma discovered that, while there was a link between price and the supply and demand of rice, the markets were strongly influenced by the emotions of traders. Candlestick charts visually represent the size of price moves with different colors. Traders use the candlesticks to make trading decisions based on regularly occurring patterns that help forecast the short-term direction of the price. Candlestick charts are used by traders to determine possible price movement based on past patterns. Candlesticks are useful when trading as they show four price points (open, close, high, and low) throughout the period of time the trader specifies. Many algorithms are based on the same price information shown in candlestick charts. Trading is often dictated by emotion, which can be read in candlestick charts. See Investopedia: https://www.investopedia.com/terms/c/candlestick.asp, https://www.investopedia.com/articles/economics/11/intro-supply-demand.asp, https://www.investopedia.com/terms/t/trading-psychology.asp, and https://www.investopedia.com/articles/trading/09/short-term-trading.asp

chart, a "Japanese Candlestick Chart," as well as Stochastics,[38] to decide when to buy a stock.

Let's summarize the process: first, asset allocation; then, sector discipline. Have a broad diversity of buy lists and buy, within the appropriate sector, the best-ranked stock with a recognizable name. Constantly think "client retention in a bad market."

Decide on a handful of fundamentally sound and highly rated companies in a sector. Choose when to buy using technical analysis. Buy at one of two points once a stock that has turned down has begun to trend up—using the candlestick charts as well as stochastics. But only when I see at least a 10 percent return up to the closest near-term resistance. The other time to buy, or more likely add more to the position, is when the stock breaks out from a period of resistance.

There are problems with this approach. Often, two people using the same chart will see different things. I joke to my staff and interns that looking at these charts is like looking at Rohrschach tests The best way to combat this is simply not to buy that day. You can always wait to do a transaction until the next day. This is the beauty of having asset-based fees and no commissions. Purchasing stock isn't a profit center. But, having the portfolios go up is!

Suffice to say that we are doing this every day—more precisely, we are going through the holdings every day, and then we are buying a few things where we have needs. Doing this is

---

38   A stochastic oscillator is a momentum indicator comparing a particular closing price of a security to a range of its prices over a certain period of time. The sensitivity of the oscillator to market movements is reducible by adjusting that time period or by taking a moving average of the result. It is used to generate overbought and oversold trading signals, utilizing a 0–100 bounded range of values. See Investopedia: https://www.investopedia.com/terms/c/closingprice.asp, https://www.investopedia.com/terms/m/movingaverage.asp, and https://www.investopedia.com/terms/o/overbought.asp.

magnified in extremely volatile markets. We have been known to run through holdings at 10 a.m. Eastern and then 2 p.m. Eastern again during those brief, highly volatile interludes.

Other drawbacks to this approach include, but likely aren't limited to, the slowness this gets fully invested in an up-trending market. If I am not convinced on the technical aspect of a stock, we just will not buy it. I remember one of my portfolio management partners[39] complaining during strong markets that it was taking too long getting the accounts invested. She was frantic that some client would call disappointed, maybe angry. I do not remember this ever happening, but it was a concern for her. Another one was that one sector would be fully invested before others.[40]

So we retain clients by simply attempting to get a market-level return with less risk. We keep the sector weightings of the portfolio very closely aligned to the sector weightings of the index. We have primarily household names, so even in a terrible market, people will recognize the names, and it will dampen their panic. We take our time getting fully invested, being stubborn about the technical aspects of the buys. What is next?

POINT TO PONDER

Just like culture eats strategy for lunch, investment process eats stock picking for lunch. Develop the process; evolve it over time.

---

39   In 2008 we began managing portfolios for other financial advisors. This has gone on throughout the last fifteen years of our career. At one point, we were managing more for others than we were for our clients. This will likely occur again.

40   Since stocks very commonly move by sector, often during that brief time period, our portfolio will have very "sector lopsided" holdings. However, this is mitigated by the fact that there would be a large percentage of cash where other sector holdings would eventually be.

RISK MANAGEMENT IN A DOWN MARKET—USING A BEAR MARKET TO IMPROVE MY RETURNS

First, let's go into definitions. Wall Street lore defines a bear market as one that has fallen 30 percent off the most recent market highs. Bear markets typically last six to twenty-four months. I've been through six bear markets in my career, and none were fun. You go to work every day fearing the next incoming call will be someone who has already decided to sell everything.

By the way, another thing that prompts those panicky client calls is presidential politics. Every time the president flips from red to blue or blue to red, there are approaching 50 percent of the population who are melancholy, and some of them panic. I have seen seemingly intelligent, business-savvy, politics-savvy, and educated clients make ridiculous blunders in these situations. Folks: it doesn't matter.

So how do portfolio managers who pride themselves on delivering index-level performance profiles deliver the goods? Remember, an index is always fully invested. If one can successfully raise cash at the early stages of a bear market and then also reinvest at the bottom, they can get this done. Sounds easy; it isn't.

First, raise cash methodically. There are multiple ways to do this, but I lean toward technical analysis again. We use two simple indicators, the 50- and 200-day moving averages.[41] If the S&P500 crosses below the 50 DMA, we like to raise

---

41   The moving average (MA) is a simple technical analysis tool that smooths out price data by creating a constantly updated average price. The average is taken over a specific period of time, like ten days, twenty minutes, thirty weeks, or any time period the trader chooses. There are advantages to using an MA in your trading, as well as options on what type of MA to use. MA strategies are also popular and can be tailored to any time frame, suiting both long-term investors and short-term traders.

somewhere in the neighborhood of 5 percent cash.[42] Sounds clear-cut, right? It is not. The number of times the cash price of the market goes below this number, does a head fake, and then crosses back above it is amazing.

If the cash price crosses below the 200 DMA, we aspire to raise our cash level to 15 percent of a portfolio. This is a big, big deal. First, it is hard to pick what you want to sell. Do you sell a position outright, or do you trim larger positions? What are the tax implications of such a trade?

A word about the tax problem. I have learned over the years that as markets go up, clients worry about capital gains. As they go down, they worry about protection of capital. Remember what I said about the hard directives the big banks force upon their portfolio managers that I do not have to put up with anymore? This will help me in the next bear market. I will be able to raise cash in IRAs unimpeded with the harsh sector disciplines required by the big firms.

The next step, which I have only had to deal with once, is when that fifty-day moving average slips below the 200 DMA. In some circles, this is known as the death star. If this occurs, we move to 30 percent cash.

Concurrent with all these things happening, we are aggressively looking for new things to buy, trying to keep our sector

---

42   I am being imprecise here purposefully. Since we manage hundreds of individual accounts, with their many differences, there could be some with more or less cash than others.

weightings intact. We are trying to essentially increase the quality of the portfolio's holdings. Example: I have always coveted owning Comcast, consistent earnings coupled with higher risk media properties. But I could never find a price that appealed to me—until the sell-off of 2020.

This is very challenging psychologically. The number of people who raise cash in the early stages, rationalizing to themselves that they will buy at the bottom, is stunning. Back to those intelligent folks who decide presidential politics dictate markets. I have had friends confide in me that they were in cash for years because "the market will go down." It will, true, but from a much higher level and not as much as you lost by selling out when you did.

The scariest thing we do is buy these stocks in a downturn, offloaded by the big institutions when mutual fund investors panic and these funds have to sell the most liquid positions. The best way to describe our technique was articulated by Jodie Foster's dad at the beginning of the movie *Contact*—"Small moves, Ellie." Don't buy 2 percent when 1 percent will do. Don't expect that great buy to be the lowest price of the stock. If it is, great, but don't go in expecting it. If it goes lower, maybe buy more. Try to be almost fully invested when the market turns up, but don't be surprised if it doesn't. Always have some dry powder. You will never, ever call the bottom.

So, to attempt to outperform the market, first, raise cash early. Second, be on the lookout for higher-quality stocks. Third, calmly and methodically improve the portfolio with an attempt to be fully invested somewhere close to the bottom. This is always a scary situation. Expect it to be. My creed: "prior preparation prevents poor performance."

OUR VERSION OF "STOCK TRADING"

There are six things that can happen when you, in one decision, sell one stock and simultaneously buy another. Five of them are bad.

Let's break this down, so you understand my rationale.

Sell one stock, then	It goes up	Buy one stock, and	It stays the same
Sell one stock, then	It says the same	Buy one stock, and	It says the same
Sell one stock, then	It stays the same	Buy one stock, and	It goes down
Sell one stock, then	It goes down	Buy one stock, and	It goes down
Sell one stock, then	It goes up	Buy one stock, and	It goes up
Sell one stock, then	**It goes down**	**Buy one stock, and**	**It goes up**

If you sell a stock and then it goes down, and then you replace it with another that goes up, this is a win; all the other scenarios are, at best, neutral. When you consider the tax implications, there are multiple new possibilities, but they are too difficult to make a blanket statement.

As such, we do not trade stocks. We simply raise cash and then, in an independent decision, buy other stocks.

POINT TO PONDER

You know bad markets are coming. Use them to improve your results.

USING OPTIONS TO REDUCE THE COST OF PORTFOLIO MANAGEMENT

First, let's be absolutely clear about one thing. Aside from simply buying very inexpensive ETFs, with which you get absolutely no advice from a seasoned portfolio manager/financial advisor, we believe we are the least expensive alternative for any client who wants professional help.

I make this rather audacious statement because there are fees everywhere, with many advisors who do not take our approach. First, if they use mutual funds or ETFs, there are operating expenses. These are very opaque, but they always exist. If someone tells you they do not, they are lying. Most advisors will justify them by saying they need the diversification. Baloney. There is a law of diminishing returns with diversification, and it soon becomes irrelevant after about forty stocks.[43] Also, note my comments above about why you should not buy non-US companies.

So, there are those pesky operating expenses. Then, there are the advisory fees. I have lived off of advisory fees throughout my career, but I'd like to believe I have provided differentiated counsel. If all you are given by your investment advisor are funky suggestions about diversifying internationally or with emerging market bonds, I fear you are not getting much valuable advice. Seems to me that the general amount charged for advisory fees centers around one percent.[44]

If the advisor you are paying does not ask for your tax returns, just what are you getting for advice? As stated above,

---

43   The law of diminishing returns also applies to diversification. While some diversification is good, particularly across several different investment sectors or asset classes, too much diversification within a particular sector or asset class is likely to have the opposite effect.

44   Advisory fee levels differ with every advisor. Our blended rate is about 0.85%.

knowing a client's tax status is imperative for providing advice. Also, family matters are important. This is where the financial advice industry seems to do rather well. Most advisors do want to make sure your family issues are well taken care of.

But I digress. For many years we have used the technique of selling call options against our clients' positions as a way to reduce their costs. Let me explain in basic terms.

Selling or "writing" a call option against a stock you hold is known as "covered call writing."[45] Here, you give some other investor, really some speculator, the right to buy your stock from you at a predetermined price[46] and by a predetermined time.[47] For us, that predetermined price must be at least 10 percent higher than the current stock price. The buyer's risk is that the price at which they buy the call option is higher than the market price on the Expiration Date. They are depending on that stock to appreciate well above the current market price and the Strike Price.

If the stock does not appreciate above that predetermined Strike Price, it was a waste of their money to purchase that option. Their possible reward, the reason they buy the right to buy that stock from you, is that if the stock price is higher than when they bought the option from you before that option expires, they make money. If that is the case, they can either buy the stock from you at that lower price and own it or sell the option with some profit.

---

45 When you write a call, you sell someone the right to buy an underlying stock from you at a strike price that's specified by the option series. As the writer, you are now short the option. You also are obligated to deliver the stock if the buyer decides to exercise the call option

46 Known as the "Strike Price."

47 Known as the "Expiration Date."

Our strategy is simply to sell the options to some other investor/speculator at a price at least 10 percent above where we purchased the stock. We want to make sure the time period in which the option expires is within sixty days of when we sold it, the price is at least 1 percent of the stock price at the time we sold the call option, and finally—going back to the Rohrshack test that is technical analysis—that we sell an option above near-term resistance.[48]

In other words, we really don't want to give up the stock! Using this formula, we have discovered that we can only find options to sell during very volatile periods and in only a few sectors. Said another way, this technique really doesn't work all the time. But generally—80 percent of the time—we bring in the proceeds from the option, known as "premium," and the option expires worthless. We keep this "option premium," which is cash. This cash input to the account is a credit against the fee we charge. This is not a sure-fire thing all the time, but there are years when we have made a big bite on advisory fees.

The mistakes we have made over the years around this technique can be described in two words: "getting greedy." For a period of time in the mid-2010s, we tried to extend our sixty-day time period to ninety days. Bad idea. We got several stocks called away from us before we realized the error of our ways. Another time the premium was incredibly rich, right at a 10 percent appreciation from the stock, but we sold the call anyway. That didn't turn out well, either. We learned to raise the

48   So in summary, there are four variables we always address: the cash price is at least 10 percent below the Strike Price; there is no more that sixty days until expiration; the Strike Price we choose is above near-term technical resistance; and we can get 1 percent of the stock's price in premium when we sell the call. A synthetic dividend.

strike price at which we sold the option to where it was just 1 percent of the stock price. This usually prevented the stock getting called away from us.

The stock got called away (in both cases). There is an old Wall Street phrase: *bulls make money; bears make money; pigs get slaughtered.* We were pigs. Thankfully, these were small positions, and we could simply wait for another buy price. Nevertheless, there were capital gains we wouldn't have had to pay.

While the above explanation seems like a no-brainer for clients, there have been many cases when clients chose not to sign option paperwork. For all the right reasons, Wall Street firms have very onerous forms that need to be signed to allow a client to use options. These exist because, in way too many cases, clients speculate with buying options and lose a ton of money. Or, they sell options and don't have a set formula like we have developed and simply lose a stock that they never wanted to lose. As you see above, we have not been perfect on this over the years, and we do it for a living.

Our approach to options isn't perfect and should be well understood by the client. If there is no understanding, they should not take this approach and just resign themselves to pay the entire fee of advice.

POINTS TO PONDER

1. *Bulls make money; bears make money; pigs get slaughtered.*
2. Options can be a great tool to reduce costs, but you must be careful.

KEY DIFFERENTIATOR: MANAGING AROUND "CONCENTRATED POSITIONS"

It is extremely common that any one investor might have one stock that is greater than, say, 10 percent of their portfolio. This can be the company where they worked for decades. It might be something inherited from a relative who has passed. It could be that they bought it, and it just went up in value over the years. They came to the advisor struggling with what to do with that stock.

Remember a few things about this dilemma. First, remember the tax consequence issue. Is this an inherited stock where selling it would literally create a massive capital gain? That circumstance should be avoided. This has happened to me on multiple occasions over the years. The stock might be sluggish and poor-performing, but that capital gain stares the client and me in the face every year. We would either trim a little off annually and replace it with companies with better growth prospects or simply work around it. We avoided other companies in the sector, so our sector weighting wasn't too out of whack.

Want a few examples of why you need to manage the weight of concentrated positions?

Think GE during the Jack Welch era. . .and then Jeff Immelt.[49]

Travelers Group and then Citigroup during the Sandy Weill era. . .and then Chuck Prince.[50]

49   In the 1990s, one of the best "sure thing" stocks was General Electric. It is clearly a household name. Under CEO Jack Welch it appreciated wildly. GE went through a thorough selection process in 2000-2001 to find the heir apparent, Jeff Immelt, who took over in late 2001. Since then, to call the stock disappointing would be a vast understatement.

50   Sandy Weill is a Wall Street legend and continues to have a loyal following amongst his past employees because of his focus growing our wealth. Yes, I am included in that group of loyal past employees. His largest mistake over the years was to pass the baton to his loyal consigliere Chuck Price. Mr. Price was not suited to the job and proceeded to demolish the stock price during his reign.

And the best one of all. . .Enron during the Ken Lay era.[51]

Manage those positions down. Not necessarily overnight. Not even over one year. But don't have the stock of any one company dominate your portfolio. Hold your nose and pay the taxes if you must.

POINT TO PONDER (AGAIN)

Don't fall in love with your stocks.

CHAPTER FIVE

PRIVATE EQUITY AND DEBT

ONE MORE TIME: there are just four investable asset classes for your serious money: stocks, bonds, cash, and real estate. Everything else you have is either a hair-splitting exercise or a derivative.

In my Occam's Razor short definition, notice I did not distinguish between public or private investments. In three of the four categories,[52] there are subdivisions that lend themselves to greater explanations.

In 1999, there were around 4000 publicly traded securities. Today there are around 2000. What happened? This shrinking of public capital markets occurred because of a piece of legislation you might remember called Sarbanes-Oxley. Go back and watch the movie *The Smartest Men in the Room* for a refresher. Enron, Ken Lay, Jeff Skilling. Sad stories all. Their sins were vanquished from the US Capital Markets from this legislation (Sarbanes-Oxley or, more formally, as the Public Company Accounting and Investor Protection Act).[53]

---

52   Public equity and private equity, public debt and private debt, and public real estate and private real estate.

53   Sarbanes-Oxley and the Competitive Position of US Stock Markets January 11, 2007

You have heard the flashy term "Money Never Sleeps," right? Well, an industry that was in the cottage phase prior to 2002 got a major boost from Sarbanes-Oxley. The private equity industry. Are the onerous filings demanded by "Sarbox" too much for your company? Go private. Are you a growing company with a vision of being publicly traded? Slow down there, big fella. Stay private for a while longer.

With this background in mind, let's refocus our attention on the investor. When Dr. Marcowitz did his seminal work in the 1950s, there were likely private individuals that invested in private companies, but these were not the focus of his paradigm-shifting research on diversification. This is simply because private firms simply are not valued on a daily basis, are not liquid, and finally, as a result of this, did not show up on his chart of an efficient frontier.

Fast forward fifty years, and numerous changes in business financing and the private equity and debt businesses are both robust and actively invested in by Americans of a certain income or net worth. The category is referred to as "accredited investor."

JUST WHAT IS AN ACCREDITED INVESTOR?

Under the federal securities laws, only persons who are *accredited investors* may participate in certain securities offerings. One reason these offerings are limited to accredited investors is to ensure that all participating investors are financially sophisticated and able to fend for themselves or sustain the risk of loss, thus rendering unnecessary the protections that come from a registered offering.

An accredited investor, in the context of a natural person, includes anyone who:

- earned income that exceeded $200,000 (or $300,000 together with a spouse or spousal equivalent) in each of the prior two years, and reasonably expects the same for the current year, OR

- has a net worth over $1 million, either alone or together with a spouse or spousal equivalent (excluding the value of the person's primary residence), OR

- holds in good standing a Series 7, 65, or 82 license.

There are other categories of accredited investors, including the following, which may be relevant to you. According to the U.S. Securities and Exchange Commission:

- any trust, with total *assets* in excess of $5 million, not formed specifically to purchase the subject securities, whose purchase is directed by a sophisticated person, OR

- a certain entity with total *investments* in excess of $5 million, not formed to specifically purchase the subject securities, OR

- any entity in which all of the equity owners are accredited investors.[54]

---

54   See www.investor.gov/introduction-investing/general-resources/news-alerts/alerts-bulletins/investor-bulletins/updated-3.

The private equity industry has witnessed enormous growth. In *The Private Equity Playbook*, Adam Coffey notes, "At the end of 1990, there were 312 private equity firms in existence. By the end of 2017, that number had grown to 5,391 firms with current assets under management totaling $2.83 trillion."

Since 2002, the private equity business has burgeoned into a major influence on US capital markets, but it is set aside for only accredited investors.

This might be the most overlooked asset class by the common, individual investor. Among the drawbacks are that, like a mutual fund, you are not in control of the tax issues. The benefit is that you need not do any work! Also, in many cases, you receive tax benefits from your ownership. Finally, you can leverage the expertise of a sponsor instead of having to rely on your own limited knowledge.

Because of its illiquidity, your potential gains in a properly structured private equity pool ought to be meaningfully higher than those of publicly traded investments, such as stocks and bonds. However, the SEC limits private equity to accredited investors for a reason; if the pool is unsuccessful, the PE firm usually has the opportunity to hold your investments for a long time. Also, expect any pool of investments to have a few losers—again, just like any other portfolio of investments.

Almost every person who meets the hurdle rates of an accredited investor and has a sufficient time horizon (of ten years) should consider having a presence in private equity. Unlike stocks, there is a paradox of choice among where to put those hard-earned dollars because of the large and growing number of private equity sponsors. Fifteen or so years ago, I sat at dinner with several Stanford University professors who suggested that you want the top four or five players to be your private equity investors for one key reason—deal flow.[55] This helps with the decision-making process.

Picture yourself as the owner of a business that you want to sell. This is a strong and robust business that generates plenty of cash for the owners. You want to sell it to someone who (1) can afford to buy it, (2) has or can get expertise to grow it, (3) is probably willing to keep you on the books for a few years while they get their legs underneath them. In more and more cases these days, this is a private equity team. The strongest ones get the most deal flow because they fit all the criteria mentioned above. This is why, as an investor, you want to skip the marginal players despite the attractiveness of their offering and stick with the biggest players.

Note that a thorough discussion on private equity is beyond the scope of this book. There are rules, fees, and liquidity issues that absolutely must be considered. For further investigation, I encourage you to read *The Private Equity Playbook* by Adam Coffey.

THIS CONCEPT ALSO APPLIES WITH PRIVATE CREDIT: WHAT IS PRIVATE CREDIT?

Let's again go back to the Great Financial Crisis of 2008. Much like the Global Pandemic, this was a near-miss on a

---

55   If you are trying to sell an asset you go first to the most likely buyer. The most likely buyers of companies are the largest, most cash-rich private equity buyers. They are also the pickiest because they have such liquidity and skills. As the investor, you want the private equity company to be shown the most deals and turn down the ones that don't precisely fit their goals. You don't want to hire the private equity buyer who is getting the leftovers.

depression. In this case, the likely depression was escaped by massive government intervention into the financial markets, then this extended into regulation.[56] You know that phrase, *banks will only lend money to people who don't need it.* This became a regulatory mantra. The term *too big to fail* plays in as well. How do you keep those enormous banks from failing? You create some massive restrictions preventing them from making too many risky loans. (I would note that banks have become as regulated as utilities.)

While this is good for safeguarding the public in times of crisis, This is bad if you are a growing business and you need a loan. If you can't get it from the banking system, where do you go? Enter private equity investors. More specifically, private credit. The private credit business has blossomed into a huge enterprise. Their ranks are filled with dozens of credit analysts and debt traders. As an accredited investor, you can invest in private credit and generate some meaningful yield on your longer-term savings.

Obviously, like private equity, there are risks. One risk, similar to private equity, is that when you join a private credit fund, you do not hand over the money immediately. Instead, you are liable to fund all capital calls.[57] My best example is personal. In the last week, I received two capital calls. There was no warning—just, "You committed to this amount of cash a year ago, now hand it

---

56   The Dodd-Frank Wall Street Reform and Consumer Protection Act was created as a response to the financial crisis of 2008. Named after sponsors Senator Christopher J. Dodd (D-Conn.) and Representative Barney Frank (D-Mass.), the act contains numerous provisions, spelled out over roughly 2,300 pages, that were to be implemented over a period of several years.

57   A capital call, also known as a "draw down," is the act of collecting funds from limited partners whenever the need arises. When an investor buys into a private equity fund, the firm makes an agreement with the investor that these funds will be available when the firm requests them.

over; we have invested it for you." Oh, by the way, we will need to hold on to it for three years, minimum. The good news? In this zero-interest-rate environment where the best you can get on a ten-year treasury is about 1.5 percent, I should be getting about 8 percent. Risk, but also reward.

One approach I encourage is that the well-hedged investor can simply use thirds as a rule of thumb to assess his weightings in these asset classes. This clearly depends on many other factors like time horizon and personal liquidity needs. If, in addition to other investments, there is a business, maybe it's 25 percent each or some balance like that. Also, given its illiquidity, let's keep the private equity down to 5-10 percent of your holdings.

POINT TO PONDER

With a few exceptions, you should be showing all of your *accredited investor* clients private equity these days.

CHAPTER SIX

MAVERICK FINANCIAL PLANNING

BOTH THE BIG BANKS and traditional financial planners seem to want all clients to have big financial planning documents. These never tend to be read and are only valid for days or weeks after the time they are produced. Seems to me this is a waste of time.

A big bank financial advisor said it again yesterday in a Zoom meeting I was attending: " I am a goals-based financial advisor." What does that mean? Goals of any type are achieved when wealth is accumulated. Accumulate wealth!

It's simple, but it's not easy.

How does one lose weight? At its simplest level, you lose weight by burning more calories than you consume. Every day, for weeks and months. Consistently.

At its simplest level, financial planning is about earning more money than you spend over a career. Every day. For weeks, months, and years. That's it!

Do not make the mistake of believing that investment returns will make up for poor spending habits. Investment returns are to insure your savings against inflation. Everything else is a bonus.

Dr. Moira Somers is the author of a terrific book every young financial adviser should read, called *Advice That Sticks*. In it, she notes, "Human Beings are hardwired to repeat actions that make them feel good. This makes us all suckers for here-and-now rewards." Convince your clients to fight that tendency, delay gratification.

POINT TO PONDER

Financial Planning is key, but don't make it too complicated.

HEALTH PLANNING IS THE SAME AS WEALTH PLANNING

It seems to me that, like many fad diets, the exercise of financial planning as it is marketed right now is in search of some magic elixir that will allow you to eat too much or exercise too little and then lose weight.

The dangerous thing about financial planning at the big banks is the bold return forecasts their "strategists" build into financial planning software; if those returns don't come to fruition, you are screwed! Isn't it better to simply save as much as possible, essentially deferring gratification to later in life, and then not worry about whether those return forecasts are too rosy?

Here's a simple approach to financial planning questions when someone is in their 50s and has a meaningful net worth.

Annual expenses < = to asset (1)*4 percent+ asset (2)* 4 percent. . .asset (n)* 4 percent.

Limitations: assets reflected above must be something

considered stocks, bonds, real estate, or the private equity equivalents—perhaps even a business investment.

This idea was formalized in the 1990s by a financial planner named William Bengan.[58] Mr. Bengen's "four percent rule" has been criticized over the years by those who suggest that that level of returns isn't sufficient because today's longer lifespans would force investors to outlive their money. My contention is that the array of investments one can use today would clearly allow for extended lifespans. In fact, investors' asset levels would grow over their lifespan, not decline.

Assumptions with a 4 percent distribution rate:

- Must use a rolling five-year period to get the 4 percent coefficient.

- Must consider taxes fully in this conversation.

Will all the assets mentioned above achieve 4 percent every year? No, but that is why we use the rolling five years.

POINT TO PONDER

Granular tax planning is the most important part of financial planning for any client who has accumulated some assets.

---

58   The Four Percent Rule is a rule of thumb used to determine how much a retiree should withdraw from a retirement account each year. This rule seeks to provide a steady income stream to the retiree while also maintaining an account balance that keeps income flowing through retirement. Experts are divided on whether the 4 percent withdrawal rate is safe, as the withdrawals will consist primarily of interest and dividends.

FINANCIAL PLANNING SOFTWARE

There is some fantastic financial planning software on the market. Like any other product attempting to achieve any specific goal, there are conditions where it is useful and others when it is not. You use garden shears to trim plants, not your nose hairs. You get it.

Financial planning software is there to solve for future goals centering upon saving for things, college, a car, a comfortable retirement, whatever. It is not, however, geared to keep you in the game in a bad market. Further, once you have acquired assets, it gives no particular insight into how to manage tax consequences around this. I'll provide an example.

Jean is my attorney. She came to me because she had a few bucks burning a hole in her pocket that she wanted to put in "an index fund." Hmmm. Jean owns a law firm. She has a couple of employees. This is money she has no need to use any time soon.

To my knowledge, no financial planning software addresses her issues. No financial planning software will say, "Jean, we recommend you set up a retirement plan for yourself and possibly employees. Make sure there is a vesting schedule, so it incentivizes employees to stay around, and if they don't, you keep the money." Again, financial planning software is no silver bullet. It is used by planners to encourage people to save more money. It is also used by most planners and big bank financial advisors to tease out more client information on their assets. These are both noble but very limited goals. Further, financial planning software is geared toward W-2 employees. Throw in a business owner with a myriad of other possibilities, and it leaves them wanting.

Another issue with this software is my concern around keeping people in the game when markets are acting angry. Most software has a line chart telling people where they will be in five, ten, twenty, or thirty years. The audacity around doing this is stunning. Life happens. Global pandemics happen, [Fill in your own personal tragedy] happens. People make decisions that change everything. You know about this: marriages, divorces, career decisions, accidents, the list goes on and on.

Piling on to this concept, when I was with the big bank, their "strategists" went through all kinds of expensive gesticulations trying to predict future returns. Most of us veteran advisors would reduce these projections to something realistic. I am suspicious that the returns were juiced up trying to demonstrate to the public that our firm was better at managing money than others. Capital market rates of return don't lie, folks. Returns are returns. These future return projections create a false sense of confidence in investors that can lead to a lack of savings over time. Again, a fad diet.

Another challenge these financial planning software programs face is how to depict making extremely forward-looking projections of markets in a fashion where the layperson—read a client—will understand and have confidence. Introduce the concept of Monte Carlo testing. Monte Carlo testing is used in many fields. It has become routine because of the cheap addition of computing power as computer computation has become less and less expensive.

The approach is to have a computer program iterate many, many different possible return scenarios looking forward for many, many years. Our problems here are the human convention, same as with bad markets we have discussed. People are irrational. While, when they look at hypothetical returns objectively, they can easily accept that someone knows better than them what might happen and what the results might be. Remember, this is probabilistic, something called Bayesian Theory.

However, when the occasional unpredictable crisis comes up, and every talking head they hear suggests that no one could ever have predicted this, and it will be different this time, they make really bad decisions and bail out. All those scientific projections go out the window.

A key area where the financial planning software fails you is in tax planning. Tax regimes tend to change every several years, and major changes seem to occur at least once a decade. Addressing these factors is where a Financial Advisor really adds value. My experience is that tax accountants spend most of their time doing, well, tax returns. They are looking in the rear-view mirror. Tax attorneys are prohibitively expensive for an annual consultation. It is the financial advisor who generally makes forward-looking suggestions based on the lay of the tax landscape. At least, this one does.

OTHER LIMITATIONS OF FINANCIAL PLANNING SOFTWARE

Now I am piling on: these fantastic software packages don't have any idea how to address your rental house, your business value, or your private equity value in any way remotely accurate. Many, many investors have, without realizing it, taken my advice and hedged their stock market investments with owning a rental, starting a side hustle business, or just having a vacation home they can turn into a rental if they need to pay for a kids education or something.

Let me be clear on my very iconoclastic point: if your client has $5 million in any kind of revenue-producing or appreciating asset, *and they can live on $200,000 per year,*[59] all that is left is dealing with taxes. If your client has $10 million, the number is, of course, $400,000. If your client is still earning an income that they can live off of, keep any big spending needs for the next six to eighteen months in cash and invest the balance longer-term in the other three asset classes. Watch—your client's liquidity and everything else will work out. It isn't that hard.

No need to care about inflation. Most long-term assets will return well over the inflation rate so long as they have an adequate time horizon.

Where financial advisors will earn extra credit is watching the tax and lending sides, and frankly, there is no emphasis on the tax side at the big banks because "they aren't authorized to discuss those issues." The loans you can get anywhere.

Doing very simplistic math using those Ibbotson charts we discussed earlier, if stocks get you 10 percent and bonds get you 6 percent over long periods of time, a blend should get you somewhere in the middle of that. If you live off of 4 percent of your investments—and you can—then reverse engineer how much income you need to how much you need in investable assets and then concentrate on tax issues. If you are already making income from a rental or another business venture you have, even better.

---

59 Simply using Ibbotson's time serries we know that a balance of stocks and bonds ought to generate a 6-8 percent return over time. Private equity and credit should be in the same range as should rental real estate.

More importantly, these side investments open up possibilities on the tax side that are very nice tools to build wealth.

POINT TO PONDER

Financial Planning Software is attractive, but if you have real estate, a business, or nontraditional investments, it really doesn't tell the tale.

USING CHARITABLE GIVING TO HELP YOUR TAXATION CAUSE

George had worked the last thirty years for a billionaire with unique types of retirement plans. Upon his retirement, he received a series of bonuses that were taxable. Some years higher than others, lasting about five years.

George was not tired of working. It became natural to take on some consulting gigs while he still had the knowledge and the connections that would earn him over seven figures during the next three years as a consultant. How could we help him on the tax issues?

Among his portfolio of assets, George had some very low basis stocks. Significant capital gains if sold. After considering multiple possibilities, we put those stocks into something called a Donor Advised Fund. The DAF, with some very clear limitations, triggered charitable deductions over the next few years that helped to cancel out the taxation on that retirement income bubble he went through.

There are other techniques you can use to achieve the same strategy. If you need an income stream either right away or sometime in the future, a charitable trust of one type or another can achieve a similar goal.

Then, there's the IRA-to-Charity approach mentioned above. All of these are worth mentioning because the tax code, as it is currently constructed, put big limitations on the deductibility of smaller charitable gifts. One must get creative.

So, how do you deal with that ever-present question of paying too much in capital gains?

POINT TO PONDER

Use charitable giving for the right reasons.
But don't forget the tax appeal.

MANAGING CAPITAL GAINS AND LOSSES

In Chapter Three, I highlighted my approach to managing capital gains. In context, using today's tax code, assets sold after one year of ownership, i.e., capital gains, pay a lower tax rate than your income or assets sold within one year of ownership. If we are trying to reduce taxes, we lean toward selling assets with over a year of ownership to reduce the tax impact.

Also, in today's tax code: if we sell assets at a loss, we can cancel out capital gains with this loss. This cancellation can extend over the years, literally for the rest of your life. So, it makes sense to take the losses, knowing at some point in your life, you can use them to cancel out your capital gains.

Note: you should be engaged with clients continuously. Part of that conversation that most advisors don't generally ask is whether the client has any loss-carryforwards from previous years on their tax returns. Ask that questions and keep track of the answer.

POINT TO PONDER

As you manage portfolios, try to also manage the capital gains.

MORE ABOUT TAX STRATEGY: GIFTING

One idea often discussed around tax strategy is gifting assets to heirs. The US tax code allows minors to get reduced or even no taxes on selling assets with capital gains. Gift to your kids or grandkids a few shares of these low basis stocks to do this. If you want to sell them at that point, please do. Remember, though, that once you gift it, it is their money.[60]

It is extremely common that parents or grandparents want to provide money, stocks, or bonds "for the child's/grandchild's education." While no one can argue that this is a sweet and kind gesture, we have run into some unintended consequences over the years.

---

60   My limited knowledge of the tax code tells me that plenty of people, with their tax preparer's blessing, will use the proceeds of these concentrated position sells to get something that is "good for the child." This is something that requires coordination with the tax preparer.

First, there have been many occasions in my career where that money gets parked in an account, or it purchases a few shares of stock (Disney and Apple are popular names). Then it sits. On many occasions, it is forgotten. In others, the place where it is purchased begins to charge fees for housing those securities and sending out statements.[61] The account gets nickeled and dimed to death.

Fast forward five, ten, or fifteen years, it is not so unusual that the now-fifteen-year-old child is struggling through high school. College and, perhaps, even technical school are not even on the radar; they can't or don't want to qualify. Having that college fund becomes a source of frustration.

Sadder yet, is when the child knows they have that money, and now it's enough to buy a small car. Grandma or even Mom does not want to give him or her that money because they are "irresponsible with money." So, it sits, ignored. I have occasions where the parents never told the kids about it, and now, they're in their thirties. What a waste!

My advice: Grandma or Grandpa do not gift that money or stock. Instead, they spend the money by adding an addendum to their will or revocable living trust, bequeathing it to the kid when they die, no strings attached. If the kid blows it, they blow it. In the meantime, Grandma or Grandpa can buy them a really good bicycle or computer or something. When it comes time for them to go to college, Grandma or Grandpa can help pay the tuition or an equally important item, like rent on the apartment.

61　This seems to be another issue with the big banks. They have these incredibly detailed statements that are "one size fits all" where even if it's a few shares of something, it gets the big statement. Then, they charge the customer for the statement! This issue has plagued clients for years.

This same scenario has come up with the ever-so-attractive 529 plan. These so-called 529 plans are sold as this great tax benefit. (It's not.) Don't do it. Keep the money and spend it on a vacation or something. Like custodial accounts, 529s are incredibly inflexible, and college can be paid for in more clear-cut ways. But beware of discussing this disrespect of 529s at the next cocktail party. My suggestion is so heretical to a traditional financial planner that you will be alienated if you bring this up! It is so contrary to the popular advice in the financial press, but it is much more pragmatic. Parents, keep control of your money! Manage the taxes proactively, don't rely on the so-called tax advantages of 529s or custodial accounts.

The more advanced approach to giving away concentrated stock holdings is known as "upstream gifting." Literally giving low basis assets to your parent or parents, with the arrangement that when they pass, their will gives that investment back to you. According to current US tax law, upon passing, the deceased's asset costs become the costs at the date of death. When Mom or Dad passes, viola, that low cost becomes the stock price on the date of their death.

The next idea to deal with a concentrated low basis position is giving it to charity. If one is used to giving, say, $10,000 to the church every year, instead of giving them cash, give them stock. The 501c3 can immediately sell it and pay no taxes, and you get a tax deduction on something you never felt you could sell because of the low cost you had of acquisition. This is a real win-win, and we have done this many times over the years.

Note: as we speak, the tax code does not provide a deduction for a $10,00 contribution in most cases. The common approach for getting around this now is to "bundle" five or more years of charitable contributions into a Donor Advised Fund and then distribute it over time.[62]

POINT TO PONDER

Custodial accounts and 529s, the irreverent truth: just say, "No."

FINANCIAL PLANNING AND INSURANCE PRODUCTS

This seems like a good time to go off on a tangent and say a few words about variable annuities. Life insurance salespeople (and other advisors) seem to consider variable annuities as the elixir of life because these instruments allow the investor to defer taxes on those investments. While this sounds noble, and I have used this myself in several situations, all it really does is create future ordinary income tax obligations. In many cases, the retired investor has to pay income tax on their IRAs or 401ks. Taking money out of annuities creates more ordinary income. This is a problem! This sometimes can double retirement tax obligations. People are coached that their taxes will go down in retirement, but if one uses all these investments that simply defer taxes until later, the marginal tax rate might not go down

---

62   According to Investopedia, "A donor-advised fund is a private fund administered by a third party and created for the purpose of managing charitable donations on behalf of an organization, family, or individual. Donor-advised funds have become increasingly popular, primarily because they offer the donor greater ease of administration, while still allowing them to maintain significant control over the placement and distribution of charitable gifts. In addition, companies are able to offer this service to clients with fewer transaction costs than if the funds were handled privately." See www.investopedia.com/terms/d/donoradvisedfund.asp

in retirement. I would much rather be deliberate about managing capital gains, knowing that there will be some years those gains need to be paid instead of pushing all of my tax impact to later in life.

Our life insurance friends also wax eloquently about the value of buying life insurance as an investment. Again, beware. I regularly hear my life insurance colleagues talk about how taking—really borrowing—money from a life insurance policy while one is still alive is a great investment. I beg to differ. I have had clients do this several times, and it has not been a great experience. First, right after the money is borrowed, the life insurance company begins sending annoying letters to the owner of the policy stating that they need to replace what they borrowed. Next, those policies you borrow money from do, in fact, charge interest on those loans. Finally, the rate of returns is marginal. Just don't do it!

POINTS TO PONDER

1. Annuities do have a place in the investment landscape, but they aren't the investment solution for everything.

2. Life insurance is only rarely an investment solution, and it is the opposite of inexpensive.

REQUIRED MINIMUM DISTRIBUTIONS AND ROTH CONVERSIONS

We have already covered our approach to using dividends and income primarily when taking RMD distributions. Our goal is to make sure most of what clients take out is dividends and interest. More can be said about that topic. This is primarily tax law rather than investment practice, but as you will see later, these two are related, and that is why the concept of "Financial Planning" is overdone in those over, say, fifty.

TWO WAYS PEOPLE TAKE MONEY OUT OF AN IRA WHEN THEY SIMPLY DON'T NEED THE MONEY

Frequently I run into situations where taking money out of one's IRA at age seventy-two is a burden for the client. They are in a position where they don't need the money and don't want the taxation. A couple of ideas should be evaluated.

If they don't need the money, and they are charitably minded, the tax code right now offers the option of giving the money directly to a charity and not paying taxes on it. This could be one or several charities, and it doesn't have to be the entire RMD.[63]

The other idea is used less often. It involves what might be described as "tax arbitrage" between the generations.

Steve is a widower. The highlight of his week is going out and playing golf with his grandsons. These boys are the beneficiaries of his IRAs. He has plenty of after-tax money in his living trust. He doesn't need a nickel of his IRAs; he is simply forced to take it by tax law.

Steve's effective tax rate is about 10 percent.

We posed the idea to Steve that, by the time he "is in a position to not care about his money," his grandkids will be in

---

63   The qualified charitable distribution (QCD) rule allows traditional IRA owners to deduct their required minimum distributions on their tax returns if they give the money to a charity. By lowering your adjusted gross income, the QCD rule can effectively reduce your income taxes.

their top-earning years and will likely have a marginal tax bracket north of 25 percent. As his IRA beneficiaries take money out of his IRA after he has passed, it will likely goose their tax rate even higher.[64]

Why not instead convert your IRA to a Roth IRA, now, Steve? It will be approaching tax neutral for you, sure, you will go from 10 percent to say 15 percent that year on your tax rate, but it will really help the boys.

First, they will never be forced to take money out of the Roth Conversion IRA we set up for them. And second, when they do choose to take it out, the distributions will not be taxed! If they want to upgrade their house or to put their kids through school, the money from Grandpa was taxed at his level many years ago.

This is the beauty of a Roth Conversion, and it doesn't apply just to Grandpa Steve; it applies to others. This year I will be able to control my taxable income, and I will likely take some portion of my IRA and convert it to a Roth.

POINT TO PONDER

A Roth conversion ought to be considered annually by the elder generation, looking at tax rates each year, as a form of intergenerational tax arbitrage.

---

64   The SECURE Act changed the rules on Inherited IRAs such that the beneficiary has to take it out ten and a half years after date of death. This change made a Roth Conversion far more tax efficient if the investor has a significantly higher tax rate than his or her heir.

CONCLUSION

This book is my attempt to tell you what I have learned about retaining clients in the combination of wealth and portfolio management. There are tons of books whose goal is to help you find new clients. There are plenty of others who will give magical approaches to portfolio management. I wanted to help you keep the clients you have because if you can hold on to them, finding new clients is just a healthy extension by simply picking up referrals along the way, and then you can hold on to them, too. Here are five concise points that will guide you.

1. Question conventional wisdom. While Modern Portfolio Theory is useful, its present form is not. There are four asset classes that meet the traditional definition of Modern Portfolio Theory: stocks, bonds, real estate, and cash. There are public and private versions of three of them. This is hard, perhaps impossible, to put on a two-dimensional chart looking for an optimal combination that shows an optimal mix. For the retail investor, taxes play such a huge part in the calculus. Don't

fall in line with the marketers, either the big bank executives or their allies in asset management. Think for yourself.

2. Fees matter. Taxes matter even more. The popular narrative from the big discounters with millions in advertising dollars is that the retail investor can do everything themselves. If they focus on fees, they solve most of their performance problems. This is patently untrue. What is true, though, is that many financial advisors have settled on doing the least amount of continuing education possible. Educate yourself. Make yourself better. This will make the fee question go away. Taxes matter more than fees. I have regularly noticed that those particularly adamant that they can do everything on their own haven't the slightest realization that the tax question is more important than the fee question. Force people to look at their tax returns. Educate them on what taxes mean to their overall wealth.

3. Don't try to be a one-stop-shop. Throughout my career, every iteration of the banks I have worked for has tried to expand their offerings into insurance and mortgage loans because they are profitable to the bank. They have hired countless specialists to help their financial advisors do this business. The results have been mediocre. Financial advisor culture doesn't lend itself to selling

insurance and doesn't include enough offerings. Insurance agents sell life, disability, and long-term care, and they are good at it! I have also seen so many disappointments when the bank forces the financial advisor to sell mortgages. Another point of confusion for the public at large around this topic is that everyone from a part-time insurance agent to an investment banker is called a financial advisor. This merely confuses the public. The different skill sets shouldn't merge together. They should get out of each other's pockets and specialize.

4. Once your clients have assets, they do not need a "financial plan," they need an asset manager managing multiple income streams, both current and deferred. They need investment advice, but not some all-knowing and all-powerful documents.

5. If the client is charitably inclined, use the tax code's charitable giving to your advantage. This goes back to my penchant for taxes being a major hindrance to building wealth. This is not to say one should not pay taxes. The tax code, in the interests of the public good, provides the individual investor ways to circumvent paying taxes to the government so long as those funds go to worthy causes. There is an amazing array of causes that are looking for funds. Find one that you like and fund it. Don't make the government do that. This will provide you with tax breaks.

The manager that first hired me into this business often said that being a financial advisor—full disclosure, back then it was an account executive or a stockbroker—was a lousy job (at times) but a great career. I echo this comment. The amount of value you can contribute to clients in your financial advisor role is only perhaps matched by their doctor. You can be a godsend to their family. You are often their most trusted advisor. Use this opportunity to improve lives and our society. Do not waste it!

ACKNOWLEDGMENTS

This book was the offspring of many parents. Each helped in different ways. First, naturally, I need to thank my family. The book was my son Ryan's inspiration, but shortly after that, both my wife Elizabeth and my daughter quickly supported the efforts. Thank you all for allowing me to sneak away—generally onto the back deck—and write on weekends instead of doing things with you.

Next, I need to thank my staff, Arnell Land and Karena Chan. The loyalty you demonstrated in forming Lattice Wealth Management with me is unforgettable. When I reflect on how much of what I wrote about in this book is what you actually do, day in and day out, it reminds me of my never-ending gratitude, respect, and admiration.

The premise of the title demanded a good grasp of how different global markets increasingly track one another. To do all of the number crunching, I was introduced to Max Grossman, at the time a graduate student at Columbia University. Max's efforts rigorously confirmed my beliefs on multiple topics. Without his work, my premise about international and US stocks in ever-increasing correlation couldn't have been demonstrated. Max completing his mission was vital to this book.

Next, I should give a shout-out to just a couple of people who allowed me to manage their clients' money. Two keys there were Alma Guimarin, who, if she ever reads this, will be surprised at the acknowledgment, but she clearly took a risk on my skillset, and I'd like to believe I delivered. Next is Casey Knowles, who also made a major commitment and trusted my team and me. While there were many others, these were two key relationships.

Finally, as I was finishing my manuscript, I went through a very methodical process to choose Scribe Media. Among other things, this involved talking to Adam Coffey, Jesse Picunko, and Moira Summers about their publishing experiences. They were instrumental in my choosing Scribe. Then I need to thank all the folks at Scribe, Erin Mellon, and Bianca Pahl. Laura Cail deserves a particular acknowledgment as she especially did some heavy lifting, scouring my amateurish work several times and turning it into something readable. Thank you one and all!

APPENDIX

Rolling 5-Year Correlations between
Annual S&P 500 and Russell 2000 Returns

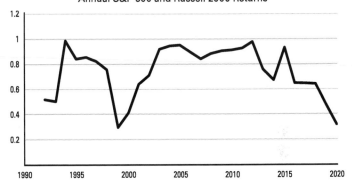

Rolling 10-Year Correlations between
Annual S&P 500 and Russell 2000 Returns

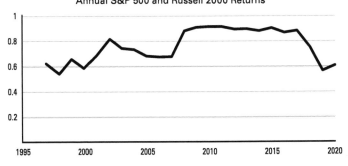

These are time series of correlations between the Standard and Poor's 500 and the Russell 2000, generally considered small-to-mid-cap US companies. These are market capitalization-weighted indices. The "Y" axis is correlation, so when the correlation is "1," these markets are moving in lockstep with each other. While there is clearly disassociation in the five-year correlations, it dramatically declines in the 10-year data series. There are two problems for American Retirees with the small cap allocations generally proposed in financial planning software. First, the allocations are very small, so frankly, why even bother. Second, investing in these smaller companies requires a level of timing that most advisors just aren't set up to possess. Again, why bother? Data in this series is from Bloomberg; charts courtesy of Max Grossman.

BIBLIOGRAPHY

1. Coffey, Adam. *The Private Equity Playbook: Management's Guide to Working with Private Equity*. Lioncrest, 2019

2. *The False Hope of Global Diversification: Confessions of a Portfolio Management Maverick.*

3. Francis, Jack Clark, and Dongcheol Kim. *Modern Portfolio Theory, Foundation, Analysis, and New Developments*. New York: Wiley and Sons, 2013.

4. Kahneman, Daniel. *Thinking Fast and Slow*. New York: Farrar, Straus and Girroux, 2011.

5. Lewis, Michael. *The Undoing Project: A Friendship that Changed Our Minds*. New York: W. W. Norton, 2016.

6. Goldman, William. *Adventures in the Screen Trade*. New York: Warner Books, 1983.

7. O'Shaughnessy, James P. *What Works on Wall Street*. New York: McGraw-Hill Companies, 1998

8. Rice, Condoleezza, and Amy Zegart. *Political Risk: How Businesses and Organizations Can Anticipate Global Insecurity*. New York: Grand Central Publishing, 2019.

9. Picunko, Jesse. *Portfolio Management for Private Wealth: An Introduction to Portfolio Theory and Practice*. Self Published, 2021.

10. Silver, Nate: *The Signal and the Noise: Why So Many Predictions Fail, and Some Don't*. London: Penguin Group, 2012.

11. Somers, Moira. *Advice That Sticks: How to Give Financial Advice That People Will Follow*. Great Britain: Practical Inspiration Publishing, 2018.

12. Soros, George. *The Alchemy of Finance*. New York: Wiley and Sons, 1987.

13. Talib, Nicholas Taleb. *Skin in the Game, Hidden Asymmetries of Daily Life*. New York: Random House, 2018.

14. Ziehan, Peter. *The Accidental Superpower: The Next Generation of Global Preeminence and the Coming Global Disorder*. New York: Twelve, 2014.